Writing Handbooks

Writing
for
Children

Books in the 'Writing Handbooks' series

Freelance Writing for Newspapers • Jill Dick

The Writer's Rights • Michael Legat

Writing for Children • Margaret Clark

Writing Crime Fiction • H.R.F. Keating

Writing Erotic Fiction • Derek Parker

Writing about Food • Jenny Linford

Writing Fantasy Fiction • Sarah LeFanu

Writing Historical Fiction • Rhona Martin

Writing Horror Fiction • Guy N. Smith

Writing for Magazines • Jill Dick

Writing a Play • Steve Gooch

Writing Popular Fiction • Rona Randall

Writing for Radio • Rosemary Horstmann

Writing for the Teenage Market • Ann de Gale

Writing for Television • Gerald Kelsey

Writing a Thriller • André Jute

Writing about Travel • Morag Campbell

Other books for writers

Writers' and Artists' Yearbook

Word Power: a guide to creative writing • Julian Birkett

Research for Writers • Ann Hoffmann

Interviewing Techniques for Writers and
Researchers • Susan Dunne

Writing Handbooks

Writing
for
Children

SECOND EDITION

Margaret Clark

A & C Black · London

Second edition 1997
Reprinted 1999
First published 1993

A & C Black (Publishers) Limited
35 Bedford Row, London WC1R 4JH

0–7136–4622–5

A CIP catalogue record for this book is available from
the British Library.

Typeset in 10½ on 12½ pt Sabon

Printed and bound in Great Britain by
Creative Print and Design (Wales), Ebbw Vale

Contents

Acknowledgements

We would like to thank the following publishers and authors for granting permission to reprint extracts from the following works:

Byars, Betsy, *The Eighteenth Emergency*, The Bodley Head, 1974

Doherty, Berlie, *Dear Nobody*, Hamish Hamilton Ltd, 1991

Hollindale, Peter, *Ideology and the Children's Book*, Thimble Press, 1988

Kingsland, Robin, *Free With Every Pack*, A & C Black, 1988

Kirkpatrick, D.L. ed., *Twentieth-Century Children's Writers*, St James' Press, third ed., 1989: Jan Mark, 'Comment' (expanded), and Chris Powling, 'Comment'

Macaulay, David and Ardley, Neil, *The Way Things Work*, Dorling Kindersley, 1988

Mark, Jan, 'William's Version', *Nothing to be Afraid Of*, Viking/Kestrel, 1980

Mark, Jan, *The Dead Letter Box*, Hamish Hamilton Ltd, 1982

Nieuwenhuizen, Agnes, *No Kidding: Top Writers for Young People Talk About Their Work*, Pan Macmillan, 1991: interview with Nadia Wheatley

Pearce, Philippa, *The Way to Sattin Shore*, Viking/Kestrel, 1983

Tolkien, J.R.R., *Essays Presented to Charles Williams*, Oxford University Press, 1947

Wilson, Jennifer, *The Signal Selection of Children's Books 1988*, Thimble Press

1. Why Do You Want to Write for Children?

Writers of children's books often complain that in the literary world they are looked down on as the poor relations of authors working in the adult field. Or rather, not poor relations but simply beginners: it's as if they are regarded as being of an age with their audience, just at the learning stage and therefore not yet ready to be taken seriously. Nothing, of course, could be further from the truth, yet I suspect one result of this patronising attitude is that many would-be writers think they can learn their craft by starting with a children's book – on the grounds that this will be easy and not much harm will be done if it turns out to be not very good. After all, it's *only* a book for children.

As a former publisher I was accustomed to reading the manuscripts submitted to us and I was often depressed by the amount of material that could be described only as 'slight' – slight in terms of content, use of language, thought put into it. Much of it clearly had its origin in the five-minute bedtime story told to a much-loved child who had all the teller's attention at the time.

Now it is true that *Alice's Adventures in Wonderland* began as a story told to three small girls on a river outing, that *The Just So Stories* were first told to a beloved daughter, that *Winnie-the-Pooh* grew out of games played with toys in an only child's nursery. But Lewis Carroll had started writing at the age of fourteen, had been published as a comic poet, and spent months working on Alice's story before it was finally published. Rudyard Kipling was well established as a poet and novelist when he decided to turn the *Just So* stories into written form (and by then the beloved child had died). A.A. Milne had set his sights on becoming a writer long before his son was born. All three were primarily *writers* and turned their skill to writing for a particular audience because of circumstance.

1

So it is important to remember, at the outset, that writing for children requires no less skill with words than writing for anyone else. Children, being inexperienced, may be uncritical readers, but they are the readers of the future and they can begin to appreciate books in the first year of their lives. It is not necessary to have children, or even like them (although this does help), to become a successful writer of books for them. It *is*, I think, necessary to be able to communicate with children and to tell a story in a way that holds your reader from page 1; it is also necessary to be able to see the world from a child's point of view, to 'gain access' – as a critic wrote of the artist Maurice Sendak – 'to emotions which for many adults are irrecoverable'.

A contemporary author, Jill Paton Walsh, has likened the experience of taking a child's viewpoint to looking at things from under the table and Beatrix Potter, writing in her sixties, put the success of her *Peter Rabbit* books down to a 'peculiarly precocious and tenacious memory', which meant she could still recall quite literally 'being seated on a crossbar underneath the library table: the tablecloth had a yellowy green fringe, and Grandmamma also had very hard gingersnap biscuits in a canister.'[1]

So writing for children does not mean writing childishly, it means writing as seriously as for adults, but with an eye to the way people and things may appear to a child. Maurice Sendak himself has explained this, when he talked about the monsters in his classic picture book *Where the Wild Things Are*:

> ...I do seem to have the knack of recalling the emotional quality of childhood, so that in *Wild Things* I can remember the feeling, when I was a child (I don't remember who the people were, but there were people who had come to our house, relatives perhaps) and I remember they looked extremely ugly to me. I remember this quite clearly, and that when people came and, with endearments, they leaned over and said 'Oh, I could eat you up!' I was very nervous because I really believed they probably could if they had a mind to. They had great big teeth, immense nostrils, and very sweaty foreheads.[2]

[1]*Horn Book Magazine*, 5, (2), 1929
[2]*Quarterly Journal of the Library of Congress*, October 1971

But in the 1990s – because society has changed so much in the half-century since World War II, with advances in technology making computers more user-friendly to most children than books – it is not enough just to be able to recall in detail your own feelings and outlook as a child. In addition to acquiring skill in the craft of writing, as well as having a story to tell or information to impart, the writer of children's books must be ready to go out and eavesdrop on children talking, to find out what topics concern them most, to discover how their perception of the world differs from that of previous generations because of what they have learnt from television and what they have *not* learnt as a result of changes in what is taught, and read, in school.

Starting point

Most publishers of children's books receive a very large number of manuscripts and what they are all looking for is a distinctive voice that is recognisable from the very first sentence. Consider the following:

> Alice was beginning to get very tired of sitting by her sister on the bank, and of having nothing to do: once or twice she had peeped into the book her sister was reading, but it had no pictures or conversations in it, 'and what is the use of a book,' thought Alice, 'without pictures or conversation?' (*Alice's Adventures in Wonderland*, Lewis Carroll, 1865)

> Roger, aged seven, and no longer the youngest of the family, ran in wide zigzags, to and fro, across the steep field that sloped up from the lake to Holly Howe, the farm where they were staying for part of the summer holidays. (*Swallows and Amazons*, Arthur Ransome, 1930)

> Imagine a tropical forest so vast that you could roam in it all your life without ever finding out there was anything else. (*A Stranger at Green Knowe*, L. M. Boston, 1961)

> 'The nicest word in the English language is holidays!' said Dick, helping himself to a large spoonful of marmalade. (*The Famous Five: Five have a mystery to solve*, Enid Blyton, 1962)

> The Iron Man came to the top of the cliff. (*The Iron Man*, Ted Hughes, 1968)

I myself had two separate encounters with witches before I was eight years old. (*The Witches*, Roald Dahl, 1983)

Once at night we watched young badgers play in the moonlight, running and racing, twisting and turning, frisking and gambolling among the trees. (*Dog's Journey*, Gene Kemp, 1996)

No matter how familiar some of these words may be now, I don't think it is hard to imagine how an editor would feel reading them for the first time. Each voice is different, in its individual way enticing, raising excitement in differing degrees about what is to come (encounters with witches? a man made of *iron*? a forest as vast as *that*? running in *zigzags*?). None (well, almost none) offers an obvious way of predicting what will happen next. The exception is, of course, Enid Blyton, whose name so many adults remember as the writer who made them readers and whose books have incurred the disapproval of so many others.

Why is it that her opening sentence, read by an adult, so depressingly predicts the holiday adventure to follow? Partly it is because she was such a prolific writer (she produced over 600 books) that the very structure of her prose, by constant use, became stereotyped. Despite her continued popularity, I think it is unfortunate that her kind of book still remains identified in many people's minds with the way to write for children. There is no one way of doing this, any more than there is one way of writing a book for adults, and for the children's writer it is vital to find your own voice from the start.

Financial rewards

The other most common misconception about children's writers is that they all make a lot of money from their books. I believe the reason is that writers of children's books are regarded as newsworthy only when they *do* make money, so the exceptions are seen as the norm. For instance, when the earnings from Public Lending Right are reported in the press there are always children's writers and illustrators in the 'top ten', but no one mentions how long it took Janet and Allan Ahlberg, Shirley Hughes or Jill Murphy to create so many of the books that children are constantly borrowing. Roald Dahl died a millionaire, but that was nearly thirty years after *Charlie and the Chocolate Factory* was first published (in New York in 1964) and he had already been writing for many years before that.

For most writers of children's books their annual income is certainly not enough to live on. According to the latest recorded statistics for new books that appeared in the first six months of 1996, about 3,600 were for children: in June 1996 there were over 54,000 children's books in print, from about 1,000 publishers. Obviously not all these books could sell at the same rate, and whereas the bestsellers may achieve sales of thousands per year, the majority of titles will be measured in hundreds. (It is salutary to think of television audiences numbered in millions.) Traditionally, children's books are priced lower than adult books; I suppose this goes back to the days when children's books were written to instruct and publishers were under a moral obligation to make them available as cheaply as possible. Recently the gap has narrowed but, again quoting official statistics, the average price of the children's books published in hardback in the first six months of 1996 was £7.19, whereas the average for adult fiction was £14.66, and for adult non-fiction £31.46.[3] The individual prices are not significant: the differential is.

Since authors are normally paid on a royalty basis, that is a percentage of the book's price, the return to children's authors is comparatively low. On the other hand, those books that become favourites with one generation will have an automatic introduction to the next, and once established a children's book can have a very long life. The seven Narnia stories, for example, written in the 1950s, must now have earned far more for the author's heirs than ever came to C.S. Lewis before his death in 1963.

There are other bonuses for a successful children's author. Even though public spending has been cut drastically in the last decade, schools and libraries still depend on holding good

[3]These figures are taken from the weekly magazine *The Bookseller*, published by J. Whitaker & Sons, which lists every new book as it appears. A cumulative list of all books in print is issued monthly on microfiche and CD-ROM and annually in book form. The microfiche and CD-ROM are available to the public in most public libraries, and most booksellers hold both for their own use.

stocks of children's picture books that can be used to encourage reading, and their creators earn both from initial sales and from subsequent borrowing. Children's book clubs are flourishing and have greatly increased both sales of paperback editions and knowledge about what is available. Parents' concern for their children's literacy has opened a new market for 'home learning' books, particularly those produced by publishers as 'own-brand' books for exclusive sale in supermarkets. The introduction of the National Curriculum in the 1988 Education Reform Act and the subsequent controversy about the books recommended for the testing of seven-year-olds in the core subject of English had at least one good effect – in drawing public attention to children's books and their authors.

If you are new to children's books, then don't expect it to be easy to find a publisher for your first effort, and don't expect a quick financial return. But if you are determined to be a writer, if you can look at things from a child's point of view without feeling that this is demeaning, if you are willing to work without much recognition from the literary pundits, then you will certainly find much satisfaction in the response from your readers.

2. Understanding the Market

Though in the eyes of the reader there may be no obvious way of distinguishing between books written for children and those written for adults (there are many kinds of both), in publishing offices the manuscripts are read, evaluated for publication, edited, promoted and marketed by quite separate departments. This is a development of the last half-century, during which much has changed in the way children are regarded, talked to, and taught. Until World War II comparatively few children's books were published of the kind we know today, although paradoxically they were given more attention in the national press. (In the 1930s they were given a weekly review column in the *Daily Telegraph*.) The popular market was then dominated by what were called 'Rewards' – stories of school and adventure bought by adults for school prizes or presents for birthday or Christmas. They had their origin in books of religious instruction of the nineteenth century, designed to improve children's behaviour and produced for free distribution to children who came to Sunday School.

The writer Geoffrey Trease, whose first book *Bows Against the Barons* was published in 1934, remembers the depression of those years and the limited boundaries of children's literature, 'when "books for boys" and "books for girls" were as carefully segregated as lavatories'.[1] The great change that brought books within the reach of children's own pockets was the introduction of Puffin paperbacks in 1941, following the launch of Penguin Books six years earlier.

The pattern of general book publishing had until then been regarded as unalterable. After first publication in hardback at

[1] 'A Lifetime of Storytelling' from *Essays and Studies*, John Murray for the English Association, 1973

an average price of 7s 6d (37½p), if an adult novel proved popular it would be reprinted in a cheap hardback edition at 3s 6d (17½p) for sale to the lending libraries. When Allen Lane proposed to lease from hardback publishers the right to reprint in large quantities (20,000 copies) ten novels in paperback editions at 6d (2½p) he was considered crazy. But his Penguin idea of bringing books within the grasp of anyone who had a thirst for them made him a millionaire and had a lasting influence on the general level of literacy. Penguins had no rival until the start of Pan Books in 1947, and Puffins were the only paperbacks for young readers until well into the 1960s.

It is surprising now to think that libraries were, until the 1970s, reluctant to buy paperbacks, partly because they did not stand up to constant borrowing, but partly because for a long time librarians did not consider them to be 'proper books'. Authors, too, were dismayed by the possibility that, if paperbacks were sold by library suppliers in strengthened bindings, then they might be deprived of the royalties they could earn from the higher-priced hardback editions the paperback was supplanting. (This is why you find printed in the prelims of a paperback, 'This book is sold subject to the condition that it shall not … be lent, re-sold … in any form of binding or cover other than that in which it is published …')

The success of the Puffin list – and its energetic promotion under Kaye Webb's editorship in the 1960s – made the paperback something children really wanted to own for themselves. They found Puffins collectable, the small format fitting easily into pockets, the small print no trouble at all, so that the paperback became a quite separate object from the solemn-faced hardback with its adult 'seal of approval'. Librarians began to soften their attitude. While public money was still in generous supply, many children's librarians bought picture books in paperback to implement their 'saturation' policy. Hard to believe, but in those carefree days if a librarian considered a picture book one that every child had a right to read, then enough copies would be bought to ensure it was *always* on the shelves (or in the book box). As soon as library funding was cut, fiction in paperback began to replace the jacketed hardback books.

So it was the consumers, the children, who really brought about the change in the balance between hardback and paperback. Publishers have to think of their customers as two groups of different people, promoting their hardback output to the adults (parents, teachers or librarians) and their paperbacks direct to the children. Sometimes this may mean a book has two different covers, sometimes a change of blurb.

Whereas for almost its first thirty years Puffin was the only paperback imprint, now almost every publisher of children's books has its own paperback arm. Some, like Faber and Walker Books, use their own names; others, who are part of a conglomerate, have a separate imprint. Red Fox, for instance, is the paperback imprint of Random House Children's Books, representing The Bodley Head, Jonathan Cape, Hutchinson and Julia MacRae Books. This has advantages for both publisher and writer: on the publisher's own paperback edition, the publisher can make a margin of profit (provided the book sells) and the writer can earn a full royalty. Where the paperback edition is produced by a second publisher under licence, the writer and original publisher have to share the revenue.

On the other hand, when there were fewer paperback imprints, some selection had already been made for the buyer and this made choosing very simple. Now that there are so many paperbacks, usually arranged not by imprint but by author's name, the buyer in the shop or the reader in the library is tempted to pick out the names that are already familiar. This makes it difficult to launch a first book by an unknown name, no matter how good the publisher may think the writer. Book clubs, and school book fairs that make up selections of paperbacks to send into schools for sale to the children, can help – although selectors are inevitably influenced by what has sold before!

During the same period that saw the growth of paperbacks there has been a change in the kind of book you are likely to find in schools. School libraries were once dismal places, with worthy-looking books locked away in glass-fronted cupboards, and the classroom housed the text books of which each child would have a copy. Certain publishing houses, notably the university presses, specialised in publishing educational books (and still do). The selling of such a book – once it was adopted by teachers – was comparatively easy. Its sale, in multiple copies, was predictable and likely to continue for years. As long ago as 1920, the publishers, led by the Cambridge University

Press, decided to remove from these books the restriction then imposed on booksellers of maintaining the 'net' price set by the publisher. Hence, educational books sell at a lower price, because the costs of distribution are less – they don't need to sit on booksellers' shelves hoping for a buyer who may not materialise. The use of 'non-net' prices spread to other kinds of books when the Net Book Agreement was abandoned in October 1995.

In the 1960s the content of the school library changed – with more funding, more emphasis on individual reading, status for school librarians (at least in the secondary schools of those days). Children's books – books of information, storybooks, picture books, written with none of the constraints of the text book – became part of school furniture. Despite the present cutbacks in book funds, books written for young children, particularly picture books, are a familiar sight in the primary school classroom where they would have been unknown only three or four decades ago.

Researching the market

If you want to write for children, you should have a look at the range of children's books now in print – and probably you could do this best in your nearest public library. Changes have also been happening in the library service. Whereas in the 1960s you would have found a librarian specialising in children's books, possibly in a room cut off from the main library, now you will find instead 'generalist' librarians who are at home equally with adults or children, lending or reference work. (A note of encouragement: according to official figures for library borrowing, while loans to adults remained static in the years 1993–1995, loans to children steadily increased.)

As you look along the shelves of the children's library, you will see how many different kinds of book are covered by this category 'for children' – as meaningless, in its way, as describing all the other books in the adjoining library as 'for adults'. The usual arrangement is by reading age: picture books, ranging from books for babies with pictures identifying one object at a time to books where text and pictures are inseparable; stories for children beginning to read for themselves; so-called 'junior' fiction; novels for teenagers. The non-fiction is likely to be divided by subject, from Art to Sport, but these books may vary in size and style from picture books for the younger readers illustrated with photographs to encyclopaedias and reference books packed with information, alongside craft books (cookery, origami) and handbooks for teenagers about fashion, social problems, health.

While the non-fiction is clearly signposted for its subject matter, the fiction is usually arranged, as in bookshops, by author's name. The adult – at least in my local library – is given much more help. If I like 'Action, Crime, Romance', or even, most telling, 'A Good Read', I can spot those books at once. I know that if I am looking for 'literary' fiction, it is under 'Fiction' I shall find A.S. Byatt. But for children there is no such labelling, even though their fiction includes mysteries, fantasies, family stories, school stories, adventure stories, historical novels, thrillers, pony stories. And it seems that they don't qualify for 'A Good Read' – perhaps because what children would find absorbing might not be what adults would want them to read.

So much is expected of children going into a library alone. They will naturally make for a book like one they have just enjoyed, identifying it by the author's name, perhaps the name of a series, perhaps a recognisable emblem on the spine (Puffin or Lion, for instance). To try something new, they need to be tempted by the enthusiasm of a trusted adult, which is why publishers and writers of children's books rely so much on the adult intermediary, whether parent, teacher, librarian or book club selector. Children can no more be lumped together in a group than can their books. They develop at different rates, have different tastes, learn to read at different ages, find their adult guide to books in different ways. Meeting the right book at the right time is very much a matter of chance.

In spite of all these hazards, the publishing of children's books continues to expand in the 1990s. The publishers listed in the annual *Writers' and Artists' Yearbook* each have a distinctive image, though this may not be easy to recognise. Each list will reflect something of the editor's own taste and most publishing houses have an individual style of design, which may show itself clearly in their picture books. If you are looking for a publisher, find one or two books in the library that appeal to your taste, write to their publishers (address on back of title page) for catalogues, and from these you will be able to judge whether what you have written may match the kind of books they publish and the style of production they use.

Another useful source of information about what is currently being published are the specialist journals that review children's books and discuss aspects of children's reading. From these you can learn what buyers are looking for, what kind of books are moving in and out of the library at most speed, how the new books are being assessed. It is worth subscribing to any of the following:

Books for Keeps 6 issues p.a. 6 Brightfield Road, Lee, London SE12 8QF. Articles, reviews, author profiles.

Carousel 3 issues p.a. 7 Carrs Lane, Birmingham B4 7TG. Articles, reviews, author profiles.

The School Librarian 4 issues p.a. Journal of the School Library Association, Liden Library, Barrington Close, Liden, Swindon, Wilts. SN3 6HF. Articles, reviews, regular select list of recent articles and periodicals on children's books and reading.

Signal 3 issues p.a. The Thimble Press, Lockwood, Station Road, South Woodchester, Stroud, Glos. GL5 5EQ. Essays and articles on all aspects of children's literature.

3. Writing for Younger Children

Most publishers are reluctant to label their children's books as suitable for one specific age, preferring to indicate the age-level by the appearance of the book – the shape or format (picture books are obviously larger than the rest), the size of type used for the text and the blurb on the flap of the jacket or back of the cover, or a vague generalised comment in the blurb. I admit, I have tried in writing blurbs to make the book appealing to as wide an age range as possible: '... suitable for all ages, but especially those who are able to tackle full-length stories on their own'; 'ideal for children who are just beginning to enjoy reading'; '... offers the least mechanically-minded reader a window of understanding into the complexities of today's technology'. This coy approach is not due to perversity on the part of the publisher; age-labelling, no matter how carefully disguised, may be very helpful to the adult buyer looking for a birthday present but it can be restricting and downright off-putting to the child reader. Who, at ten, would want to be seen even picking up a book marked '527'? (This numbering was meant to be intelligible only to the adults, but it was only the adults who did not understand it.) A children's librarian, asked 'What do ten-year-old boys read?', replied that the only answer she was prepared to give was in the form of another question, 'What do forty-year-old men read?'

It is, anyway, almost impossible to match a child's reading age with that same child's literal age, and children read – as adults do – on many levels at different times. Joan Aiken, a writer of plays and thrillers as well as children's books, once said:

> It is impossible to predict what a child's mind will seize on at any stage. Their minds are like houses in a staggered process of building – some rooms complete with furniture, others just bare bricks and girders.[1]

[1]*Books*, vol. 2, National Book League, 1970

13

In their catalogues, however, publishers have to categorise their books in rough age groups. The catalogue, after all, is their main selling tool: the means by which they announce to their customers the books they have in stock (and their prices) and the new books that are coming. The categories most commonly used are: picture books, including board books and other 'novelty' books, for the youngest (that is, 0–7), stories for the beginning readers (5–7), longer stories for confident readers (7–10), stories for 'middle' children (8–11), fiction for older children (9 up), novels for the sub-teenage readers (10 up), and novels for the teenager (13 up). Then there is non-fiction, divided roughly between younger and older children – and by now you can probably guess that younger turns into older round about eight or nine. But the categories constantly overlap. Raymond Briggs' *When the Wind Blows* (how 'the decision made by the Powers That Be will get us in the end') is a picture book for teenagers or adults, certainly not the toddler. And 0–7 is no mistake. Parents and educationalists now say it can never be too early to start reading to children, and babies can start looking at picture books, pointing to words and pictures, long before they can talk. If you want to find out more about this, read Dorothy Butler's *Babies Need Books*.

Some basic guidelines

One of the commonest misconceptions about writing for younger children is that, to tell a simple story, you are restricted to the use of one-syllabled words ('The cat sat on the mat') and you must explain everything in minutest detail. To write simply means thinking seriously, choosing every word with care, then cutting away everything that is unnecessary to an under-standing of the basic plot. This is made easier in a picture book, when much of the story will be told through the illustrations. The classic example is Pat Hutchins' first book, *Rosie's Walk*. The writer here is her own illustrator, but the book began with words – a long story set in a farmyard, which (Pat remembers) 'went on and on'. Each of the animals made its own noise, except for the fox who came in at the end, saying nothing. The publisher to whom the manuscript was shown saw in it the possibility of bringing out the humour of this mute fox by showing him getting the worst of all the potential disasters in a walk round the farmyard. After much collaborative work between writer and editor, the text was pared down to just thirty-two words, in which the fox is never even mentioned. He appears only in the pictures. *Rosie's Walk*, first published in 1968, has become a classic favourite with the very youngest. But ideas, says Pat Hutchins, are never wasted. They stick around in the back of your head and suddenly emerge in different shape. Those noisy animals who got in the way of Rosie and the fox finally made their voices heard in *The Little Pink Pig*, Pat's twentieth picture book, published in 1994.

The choice of words is equally important. Speech is usually spontaneous and careless, but writing involves thought. Telling a child of four about Robert, my dog, I said, 'And Robert ate a whole bowl of biscuits', to which she replied without a pause, 'Did he eat the cup and saucer as well?' If I had been writing that sentence, I hope I would have phrased it as 'Robert ate all the biscuits in his bowl.' The child had been concentrating intensely on exactly what I was saying, and although she did not consciously know this, she had already grasped the idea that the word 'ate' was a verb and that it governed the noun that followed it.

Writing is such a private activity that I don't believe formal rules can, or should, be imposed on the writer, but if your meaning is to be clear (and this is all-important with children) your sentences should be constructed according to basic grammatical patterns. A teacher of English Literature, now long forgotten and out of fashion, gave the following advice in the belief that 'the more clearly you write the more easily and surely you will be understood ...'

1 Always prefer the concrete word to the abstract.
2 Almost always prefer the direct word to the circumlocution.
3 Generally, use transitive verbs, that strike their object; and use them in the active voice, eschewing the stationary passive, with its little auxiliary *is*'s and *was*'s, and its participles getting into the light of your adjectives, which should be few.[2]

[2]Sir Arthur Quiller-Couch, *On the Art of Writing*, CUP, 1916

He goes on, in the sexist phraseology of his time, 'For, as a rough law, by his use of the *straight verb* and by his *economy of adjectives* you can tell a man's style, if it be masculine or neuter, writing or "composition".' I can't think of better advice for writing directly and with clarity. Participles and adjectives should be used in moderation, especially the participle unrelated to the subject of the sentence. When a politician says, 'Having said that, the economic situation will improve', he is misusing the participle 'having said' in order to avoid phrasing the sentence, 'Having said that, *I think* the economic situation will improve ...'

When you are writing for children, make sure that every word counts, and that all your words match as closely as possible what is in your mind or imagination.

Picture books

I do not know how children learn to speak in sentences rather than mouthing one word at a time, but I do know that it is never too soon – in terms of the age of your child audience – to give a shape to the story you are writing for them. No matter how simple the tale, it should have an enticing beginning, an enthralling middle and a satisfying end. If it is a small domestic drama, it can be given the structure of something as obvious as the timetable of a young child's day, or the putting on of outdoor clothes for an expedition to the park paralleled by the removal of the clothes on the return home.

The physical make-up of the picture book imposes limitations on both writer and illustrator, but this can also be a help in shaping the story. All books are printed on very large, flat sheets of paper divided into pages arranged in such a way that when the sheets (printed on both sides) are folded and trimmed they make up a book of pages in the correct order. When a book is illustrated with pictures in colour, these sheets go through the printing machine four times so that first yellow, then magenta (red), cyan (blue) and black inks can be applied, one on top of the other, to reproduce the artwork. The sheet is divided into multiples of eight pages, the most usual being sixteen pages on each side, producing a book of thirty-two pages in all. At the front and end of the book will be the 'end-papers', sometimes printed in a plain colour, sometimes decorated with an illus-tration. Two more pages will be taken up by the title-page, with title, author's and illustrator's names and the imprint of the publisher, and the page facing or following the title-page, which will contain the copyright notice, the name of the printer and bibliographical information. That leaves twelve 'openings', that is two pages facing each other, for the story. Ideally, each of these double-spreads should be complete in itself, like a mini-chapter, representing a stage in the story, sometimes ending with a cliff-hanger ('and round the corner was a ...'), the text always moving the plot along while the illustrations show what the text can't (and sometimes even showing another story moving in parallel), each needing the other to make a perfect whole.

Some of the best picture books have been created by artists who can also write their own texts, but publishers are always looking for new ideas and original stories to make into picture books. A publisher will be better able to consider your work if you show an understanding of how a picture book is produced, and if you have already considered how to break up your story into passages that will give the illustrator opportunities for filling in the background to the story, for developing characters who are merely names in the text. Do not worry about finding an illustrator yourself; publishers usually prefer to do this and may already have a budding illustrator waiting for the right text to turn up.

Writing the text for a picture book is an art that demands an ear for words and a feeling for the rhythm of a story that can be read over and over again with no lessening of satisfaction. Look at the text of Maurice Sendak's *Where the Wild Things Are*, read it aloud, think about whether it could be told in any other way.

What makes a good story?

But before you start writing, before you begin even to plan the shape of your story, there has to be an idea. Whether it is going to make the simplest of books – the naming of single animals or things, for instance, linked by numbers (a counting book), or by letters (an alphabet book), or by a question ('Where is ...?') – or a story in which events follow one another in chronological order, it is the *idea*, the point of the book that matters. Often the only reaction to a manuscript has to be 'So what?' and I am sure the reason is that the writer has not thought it necessary to develop an idea to the stage where it will stand up to a child's serious scrutiny. Another common misconception about writing for children is that children's lack of experience makes them incapable of understanding. Do not take my word alone for this: here is what the experts say. Dorothy Butler, a teacher, book-seller, mother and grandmother, writes, 'A truth that is still over-looked, or at least undervalued, is that what a child understands is much more important than what he can express at a given time.'[3] Liz Waterland, a teacher and mother, who believes in teaching children to read with 'real' books rather than reading schemes, applies this test when selecting books: 'Can the story,' she says, 'however simple, be read aloud by an adult in a natural, interested manner and without sounding patronising?'[4]

Ideas can come from anywhere at any time. Writers tell me that 'thinking time' is important, and even if it is not possible just to sit looking out of the window, you can let your mind go blank over the washing-up and you may be surprised what comes into it. If you sit in front of your typewriter or word processor thinking 'I'll write about a girl and a baby brother and a cat' you will probably soon get bored or stuck. You have to wait until a particular girl comes into your mind and 'grows on you' as you think about her, consciously or unconsciously, until one day you hear her speaking. This may sound fey or pretentious, but from what many writers have said I am convinced that the creative process is the same whatever kind of fiction you are writing. If you do not care enough for your characters to know more about them than you are actually putting into words, then it will show, and your readers will not warm to them either.

Traditionally, the subject matter of picture books is based on nursery rhymes, fairy tales, folk tales, animal fables, and the everyday happenings that are the source of continually exciting discoveries in a child's world. Patterns for the rhythm and

[3]Dorothy Butler, *Babies Need Books*, 1980
[4]Liz Waterland, *Read with Me*, 1985

repetition that make a text so appealing to read and to hear can be found in folk tales like 'The Gingerbread Man', where a constant refrain accompanies a chase, or the cumulative story, of which the best known is perhaps 'The House that Jack Built'.

One of the best examples of a picture book that is as simple in its structure as it is ingenious as an idea is *Each Peach Pear Plum* by Janet and Allan Ahlberg. Allan Ahlberg was the writer and Janet the illustrator, but their work is inseparable. 'Between us we bat ideas back and forth like a game of ping-pong,' Allan said in a *Sunday Times* interview for 'A Life in the Day of ...' (Sadly, their perfect partnership was broken by Janet's tragically early death in 1994.)

Each Peach Pear Plum is a picture book of thirty-two pages. In this case the end-papers are separate – you will find there are many variations in the make-up of a picture book, but the basic factor, a multiple of eight pages to a printed sheet, remains the same. The format is landscape – that is, the width is greater than the height of the book. This is one aspect of the book that must be decided at an early stage in discussion between editor, art editor, illustrator and writer, for the shape of the book can be important to the composition of the pictures.

The theme of this book, and an instruction about how to 'read' it, are explained in four rhymed lines on page 1:

> In this book
> With your little eye
> Take a look
> And play 'I spy'

On pages 2 and 3, which also include the title of the book, there is a picture of the inviting green landscape where the story is set: a cottage, an orchard, a hill behind it, a bridge over a stream. Each of the fourteen double-spreads that follow are arranged in the same pattern: on the left-hand page two lines of rhymed text set in large type, on the right-hand page a framed picture, full of detail. The rhymed text introduces one nursery-rhyme character after another, the second always carefully hidden in the picture on the right. Beginning with

> Tom Thumb in the cupboard
> I spy Mother Hubbard

the reader is led through the cottage, up the hill, over the bridge, back to the orchard, where under peach, pear and plum trees all the characters come together to eat Plum Pie.

Each spread is complete in itself, for adult to read aloud while child (in arms, on knee) concentrates on the picture in the search for the three bears (half seen through a window) or Cinderella (whose feather duster waves behind the paraphernalia in the cellar) and picks up a story that develops in the pictures but is not mentioned in the text. *What* will happen to Baby Bunting floating down the stream?

If you look closely at *Each Peach Pear Plum* you will see why a child, absorbed in the pictures, would want to go back to the beginning the minute it was ended, and why children beginning to read for themselves still find it beguiling.

Animals as characters

Just like nursery-rhyme characters, animals are a useful substitute for human characters in picture-book stories. If there is in your mind a very difficult character who will not cooperate, who is awkward and won't go to bed, then it may suit him or her to be a hippopotamus rather than a recognisable child. Then the child reader can participate in both deploring the hippo's anti-social behaviour and secretly enjoying the joke of identifying with a character who couldn't possibly be himself.

At the same time, I think the animal character only works if it retains some of its natural habits as well as assuming human feelings. In retelling Aesop's fable, it seems permissible to give the tortoise a more lively personality than that of the natural plodder, but the point of the story is lost if the tortoise starts to run. And, as one editor told me (who also happens to be chairman of his firm), before your animal character opens his mouth to say good morning, you must know quite a lot about him – whether he's an optimistic character who sleeps well but wakes early, what he had for breakfast (this should be in keeping with his animal habits), whether he has friends, whether he likes books, what he enjoys doing most. None of this need be spelt out in the text, but you must know it before you can make him convincing.

Bears, mice and rabbits seem to be especially popular as book characters, and a most endearing pair, Big Bear (father) and Little

Bear (son), are the protagonists of three picture books written by Martin Waddell and illustrated by Barbara Firth. They are all books that could be shared by an adult reading aloud while a child of two or three looked at words and pictures, and could also be enjoyed at home or in school by children of five or six learning to read alone. They demonstrate the advantages of using animals in childhood experiences that children of many ages share.

The first book (in order of publication), *Can't You Sleep, Little Bear?*, is a story of bedtime in the hours before sleep comes, when the baby can only be comforted by being picked up and shown the moon in the sky. The book won both the Smarties Prize[5] for 1988 and the Kate Greenaway Medal[6] for its illustrations. Writer and illustrator were therefore faced with the challenge of producing a second book about the same characters – a challenge common to writers of all kinds of books. Do you let your characters grow up? Do you change the setting? Do you duck the challenge for fear of repeating yourself? In this case the theme of the second book extends the experience and surroundings of the baby bear, while offering the same opportunity for question and answer between the two characters and a satisfying story line that ends in the warmth and comfort of HOME.

Let's Go Home, Little Bear is about coming home from a walk – that first venture very young children make into the world outside home. Because father and son are bears, they walk in the woods, thus providing an even clearer image of the vast, unknown territory outside the cosy, safe security of home. And being bears, they walk in the woods alone; as Barbara Firth draws them, they walk on their hind legs, stand in human attitudes and make appropriately human gestures to one another, but they don't wear clothes and aren't encumbered with any impedimenta like a buggy. They are bears, with human personalities.

[5]Until 1996 an annual prize of £2,000 each in three categories (0–5, 6–8, 9–11), and an additional £8,000 for the best of the three, sponsored by Smarties. In 1996 the rules changed to allow for three prizes in each of the three categories: Gold (£2,500), Silver (£1,500) and Bronze (£500), with no overall winner
[6]An annual prize of no monetary value for the best illustrations to a children's book, awarded by the Library Association of Great Britain

The large format of the book is portrait (that is, the height is greater than the width) and has plainly been chosen to suit the upright stance of Big Bear, as you can see from the cover. The end-papers are not printed but are made of coloured paper (a warm coral, to contrast with the snowy background of the pictures) so the thirty-two pages are devoted to, first, the dedication (the writer dedicates the book to its editor and art editor), then the title-page, followed by the story (of just under 700 words) which is carefully structured, double-spread by double-spread.

The story begins in a traditional way, repeating the first four lines of the first book, introducing the two characters to new readers and reminding those who already know them:

> Once there were two bears.
> Big Bear and Little Bear.
> Big Bear is the big bear
> and Little Bear is the little bear.

The text is deliberately broken into short phrases, each on a separate line, with wide spacing in between, to help both the adult who is reading aloud and needs to pause now and then, and the child who is reading silently. (For more about book design, see pp. 84–7.)

Then the new story starts: 'They went for a walk in the woods.' In the picture we see Big Bear (very big, three times the size of Little Bear) walking beside L.B. who is almost prancing along, but concentrating, eyes down. The next page has only two sentences:

> They walked and they walked and
> they walked until Big Bear said,
> "Let's go home, Little Bear."
> So they started back home on the
> path through the woods.

Here you can see how the writer is looking at the scene from the baby's viewpoint. The text may seem simple and artless, but notice that it doesn't say 'They walked a long way': at L.B.'s height he can see only a few steps ahead, so distance is meaningless. A few steps from home can be as remote as the North Pole. Nor does the text say 'They walked for a long time'. L.B.

does not yet have a sense of time. No, the repetitive phrase is used for its precise appropriateness to L.B.'s feelings as well as its rhythm.

Now comes the drama in the story. Three times L.B. stops, listens, turns round and looks. Three times B.B. says 'Come on, Little Bear,' and each time, using the same words, L.B. tells what he has heard. First, 'Plod, plod, plod, I think it's a Plodder!' Next, 'Drip, drip, drip, I think it's a Dripper!' and so on, with B.B. providing the reassuring explanation. Until ... L.B. is so tired, he has to be carried. On his father's shoulders, he hears new sounds at this astonishing new height, the WOO WOO WOO of the wind, the creak of the trees. Safe home at last, B.B. gives a reprise of the drama when asked for a bedtime story and on the final page both bears are shown fast asleep, above the one word (in large capitals) HOME.

What is left out of the text is any suggestion that L.B. is frightened by the sounds he hears. That response will be supplied by the reader, as the page is turned to reveal why L.B. has stopped, listened, turned round and looked. The repetition of the words is important to the build-up of the excitement as each new sound is explained, observed in the illustration, and understood. And the sounds – here the single syllable is vital for even the youngest to copy – are such that babies still too young to understand the explanation will enjoy them.

The third book, *You and Me, Little Bear*, again uses the familiar, four-line opening, and takes Little Bear one step further on the round of everyday living. Though not noticeably much bigger in size, L.B. now knows that 'playing' is more fun when B.B. joins in. Playing and working together is the theme of the story – an admirable example of re-using characters who have proved popular and successful while remembering that the *idea* behind any sequel has got to be as good as the first.

Shaping the text

Chronicling the discoveries and happenings of a child's first years is one way of writing a picture-book text, whether you make your characters animals or real children, as Shirley Hughes does in her books about Alfie, or the classic *Dogger*, about a favourite toy that's lost and found. (This idea came during a spring clean, when a once-loved soft brown toy dog fell out of a cupboard.) At the other end of the age-scale the plot of a comic-strip picture book about Asterix or Tintin, *Fungus the Bogeyman* or *Gentleman Jim*, can be complex. Such books, where the text can be filled with verbal jokes that are satirical, sometimes subversive, and often esoteric, are appreciated by older children or teenagers, although a favourite picture book with younger children, *Father Christmas* by Raymond Briggs, makes use of the cartoon technique and all the text is in 'bubble-talk'.

In picture-book texts for these younger children a plot is not so important as a unifying element that links one double-spread to the next. This can be a single, identifiable character (look at *Cloudy* by Deborah King, about a cat), or a period of time (a book that tells its story in pictures alone, *Sunshine* by Jan Ormerod, describes early morning for a small girl), or a place (in John Burningham's *Oi! Get Off Our Train*, it's the train that brings together a crowd of endangered animals as it steams through a dream landscape).

Putting words to your basic idea means first giving it a shape and then thinking about what is best shown in the pictures and what can only be conveyed by the written word. There is no need to worry about vocabulary, apart from being meticulous about choosing the right word for its *meaning*. Although, when using dialogue, you must match the way people talk to one another, the text will be written for reading, and reading aloud, again and again, so the expendable words that you would use when talking or chatting – the waffle that starts a conversation – must be cut out. (I think we have all learned that children can distinguish, quite early on, the words flying about carelessly in chit-chat from the words in the picture book that are always in a special order.) The way adults talk to children now is very different from the way it used to be, and this applies equally to writing for them. If you listen to the voice of broadcasters in the 1940s you will find the tone of condescension unmistakable, but happily this has disappeared – though I detect a touch of it in the very phrase 'writing *for* children'. In an essay under that title, the poet Eleanor Farjeon gave this pertinent advice:

Cast out of yourself the notion that 'children' are a sort of static group that can be written 'for' en masse. Otherwise, you will be addressing an imaginary audience, and aiming at a bull's-eye in a non-existent target.[7]

Try to avoid 'writing down' to your audience; concentrate on trying to see things from their viewpoint; treat your young readers seriously rather than addressing them as if they were a group of people different from or inferior to yourself.

If you have an idea for a book that comes into the 'novelty' category – a pop-up or a lift-the-flap, a book to sniff or to feel – you can submit it to a publisher purely as an idea, and if the publisher thinks it a good one you will be invited to discuss ways of developing it. Pop-up books, for example, need the skills of a paper engineer.

Stories for beginner readers

There has been much public debate about how children are taught to read, and there is controversy among educationalists about the use of picture books, and books produced for children by general publishers, in preference to reading schemes, the series of graded text books produced for this purpose by educational publishers. Whatever the outcome of the debate, it seems likely that many teachers work with a mixture of the two kinds of book. While the reading schemes are written to strict rules by specialists, both teachers and parents are aware that stories for beginner readers, produced with large print and illustrated on every page, are a useful supplement to the reading scheme because they encourage children to become readers by showing that the pleasure they derive from picture books and stories told to them can be achieved from words read at their own pace and under their own control.

The use of picture books in teaching children to read and the demand for books in which the text begins to play the major role have led to a proliferation of series for the beginning

---

[7]'Writing "for" Children' from *The Writers' Desk Book: A Comprehensive Guide to the Various Aspects of the Writer's Craft*, A & C Black, 1935 (reprinted in *Signal*, May 1993)

reader. Most publishers now have at least one series, or group of books, devoted to this kind of story: Sprinters from Walker Books; Blue and Yellow Bananas from Reed Children's Books; Crunchies and Super Crunchies from Orchard, and so on. You will find all the series listed in the *Writers' and Artists' Yearbook*. The books are produced in a series style, and usually to a uniform length, and publishers are always looking for new material. It is worth having a good look at some of these series, to see whether one of your ideas might fit into this category. You should find a selection in your public library, where they are likely to be grouped together, in order of author, under 'Beginner Readers'. They vary in length from a few words to a page to a total of 2,000 words or so.

This area of children's publishing will continue to grow, I am sure, with the current concern about literacy and the use of the Standard Assessment Tasks for the National Curriculum for Reading. The Schools Curriculum and Assessment Authority issues annually a list of recommended reading books and texts for testing young children's reading attainment.

This stage of reading may not last long, however, only until the child is fully confident of moving on to a longer narrative. Much of the material may therefore be ephemeral, but it is important, being the first introduction to print that can be read by the child alone.

One writer's experience

Chris Powling is both a teacher and a writer. One of his stories for beginner readers, *Bella's Dragon*, illustrates the chief features of this genre. It has a simple but satisfying, and shapely, plot: a fire-breathing dragon wants a change of scene; Bella's school is closed because the boiler has broken down; boiler-room becomes dragon's den. Reality and fantasy are mixed in a way easily understood by children, both in the text and the line drawings that break up the text on every double-spread. The story moves quickly through the course of one day, and the text mostly takes the form of dialogue. This is how it begins:

> On the coldest day of the year, a dragon suddenly flopped into Bella's back garden.

The approach is direct and spare, with no need for any description of Bella, whom you see in the illustration above this opening sentence, so you know she is black, and just the height of the window-sill. She immediately says 'Hello' to the dragon, so it's obvious she is a friendly child, and it's likely the reader will warm to her because she is kind and resourceful when the dragon appeals to her for help. But nothing of what I am explaining need be stated: it is all implicit in the dialogue.

The story is, in adult terms, no more than an anecdote, but it is told with the same regard for pace, for building up the dramatic tension, as an adult would use in entertaining a group of friends with a 'good tale'. Although the text is not divided into sections, there are stages in the progress to its conclusion. Bella does not find the answer to the dragon's dilemma straight away; there are solutions that prove disastrous and at each stage a kind of refrain is repeated: (of the dragon) 'It's one of those big, electric toys, isn't it? Or a computer-robot thing?' There is no obvious restriction on vocabulary, but participles and meandering description are scrupulously avoided. In every other respect, apart from its length (2,000 words), it's a real book that's worth reading.

The idea, Chris Powling says, came to him when the boiler in his school went out and the janitor brought it to life with a kick, muttering, 'Get on with you, you old dragon!'

About children, this writer says,

> For me what matters most in my work is plot, humour, and a narrating voice as close as the text allows to that of a storyteller improvising out loud about his/her characters. If I can also capture something of the freshness, enthusiasm and ruthless honesty of children at their best, so much the better. Children see the world from the viewpoint of someone who hasn't lived very long … and it's not a bad viewpoint. Certainly none of us becomes so wise we can afford to dispense with sheer astonishment at existence and what it entails. This is why writing for children seems to me to be just as serious as writing for adults – and a lot more fun.[8]

---

[8]*Twentieth-Century Children's Writers*

Series publishing

Some reviewers are very critical of series publishing, and the quality of books published in a uniform style can be very uneven. Both publisher and writer can easily become lazy, knowing that it's likely each book will sell on the reputation of the series as a whole. But readers are often comfortable with a series, confident that if they have enjoyed one book (or found it within their reading capability) the next will be the same, enjoyable and well within their grasp. There are other, practical advantages – books of similar length and similar page-size can often be printed together, as can the covers, and this may save money in production costs, particularly with the printing of colour.

The series, therefore, can be a useful way of launching a new writer whose name is not yet known. Buyers and readers are often unwilling to try a book by someone they have not met before, but in the context of books by other writers they trust they can be enticed into looking at something new. In an ideal world booksellers, librarians, teachers and all those adults responsible for introducing books to children would have the time and energy to read and assess every book as it was published and recommend it (or not) to the readers by word of mouth. But there are far too many books for this to happen and when it does, it takes time – and time is another factor of importance in the publishing process, for books must keep moving out of the publisher's warehouse at the same rate as they are going in. (See p. 87 for further explanation.)

Robin Kingsland had never had anything published when he submitted some short stories and a single poem to the Children's Book Department of A & C Black. He'd selected the publisher from the list in the *Writers' and Artists' Yearbook* – and perhaps Black were lucky to come so near the beginning of the alphabet. (The book business is full of such chance encounters and the alphabet is often responsible for a reader's choice of book. Lucky those writers whose names ensure their books' place on the eye-level shelves of library or bookshop!)

The material was read (as is everything submitted to a reputable publisher) and one line from the poem stuck in the editor's head, prompting her to suggest a meeting. Writer and editor discussed a new series, Jets, then (nearly ten years ago) at the planning stage, intended for children who'd gone through the 'beginner' period and were now independent readers. Writer was given the simplest of briefs: to prepare a story line (a synopsis) for a book of 2,000 words, divided into chapters, with illustrations on every page integrated with the text (that is, forming part of the text, rather than drawn as separate pictures). Writer produced three ideas, all of which were accepted, and writer was encouraged to go ahead with both text and illustrations, on the understanding that the latter would be subject to the editor's approval.

All this took about a year, which may seem a long time for a book of only 64 pages, but publishers know that they must have new writers and that writers need to see their work in print, to have the experience of being published, if their writing skill is to grow. Here was a writer whose ideas and talents needed the kind of nurture that an editor could provide.

Free With Every Pack – the first of the three stories Robin Kingsland wrote for the Jets series – is really a Dick Francis novel in miniature, a story of kidnap and rescue that is full of chills and thrills, but told with humour, so that even a 'newly independent' reader would instinctively know this is not a story of something that could really happen but a form of story that gives you a tingle of excitement and simultaneously makes you laugh. Each page has illustrations drawn in comic-strip style with much of the dialogue in bubbles. The plot demands concentration, for the story starts *after* the kidnap, so there has to be a flashback to the wicked early life of the kidnappers, and there are several characters to keep clear in your mind (though they are transparently good or bad). The writer uses puns ('Oh, he's a hardened criminal,' says the policeman as the villain is led away encased in cereal honey coating), jokes ('Stig Stubble had been a criminal for as long as he could remember. Which wasn't very long – he didn't have a very good memory.') and set phrases from the thriller genre ('... and the pride of the local police force swung into action') that even a new reader would recognise for what they are – all with such verve that an adult would not be embarrassed to read the book aloud.

So if you receive a letter from a publisher rejecting your manuscript but suggesting that you might think instead about another project, be prepared to put your first idea aside for the moment. Editors can be very helpful, and if you are daunted by the thought of an expensive journey to London (where most publishers are based) say so! There are ways round every obstacle if you are really determined about what you want to do.

Moving on

In publishers' catalogues and in libraries you will find another group of books sometimes defined as 'Moving on', sometimes as 'Young fiction', aimed at the reader on the next step between learning to read, becoming an independent reader and acquiring the stamina to stay with a book of 100 pages or so. If pressed to put an age to this category most publishers would say 'seven to ten'.

This stage of reading is, again, dominated by series – mainly because illustration is still important and, as already explained, prices can only be kept within reasonable bounds by printing books of similar size and length together.

One of the oldest and most enduring series is Hamish Hamilton's Antelope series for which Jan Mark wrote *The Dead Letter Box*. Jan Mark started writing when still at school, but it was several years before her first book for children was published as a result of winning a competition organised by Penguin Books and the *Guardian* newspaper. *Thunder and Lightnings* subsequently won the Carnegie Medal[9] for 1976 – so it is always worth looking out for writing competitions.[10]

Jan Mark has an ear for children's conversation and learned a lot about their behaviour while teaching, particularly when encouraging children themselves to write. She uses the technique of giving children postcard reproductions of works of art and then asking them to write a page of a story (not the beginning) to match it. This is an excellent writing exercise for any age.

In *The Dead Letter Box*, her story of about 7,500 words is divided into six chapters and illustrated with line drawings that support rather than expand the text. The pace is not hurried.

[9]An annual prize of much prestige but of no monetary value for an outstanding children's book, awarded by the Library Association of Great Britain
[10]In 1993 the *Independent* newspaper and Scholastic Children's Books launched an annual competition (usually announced in the paper about March) for short stories for six- to nine-year-olds

The reader is enticed not to follow a rapidly moving plot but to become curious about what will happen to the friendship of Louie and Glenda when Glenda moves house. The text makes you think about what the words imply as well as what they mean literally. Here, in the first paragraph, a metaphor creates the image of the lamp post in Glenda's garden:

> For five months now there had been a FOR SALE sign outside Glenda's house. Louie hardly noticed it any more; it had become part of the garden, like the concrete goblins, the bird-bath, and the green lamp post which grew up through the hedge; a tall tin plant with an orange flower on top that bloomed only at night.

No picture helps you on the first page: you are on your own with the words. The dialogue, when it comes, is crisp:

> 'You've sold your house,' Louie said, when Glenda came out through the gateway.
> 'Last week,' said Glenda. 'They only changed the sign yesterday.'
> 'You never told me.'
> 'I forgot.'

And the reason becomes clear when you read that 'Glenda and Louie were best friends, but Glenda was Louie's only friend, while everybody was Glenda's friend.'

The reader's world is expanding to include not just what happens to the characters but what they are like as people and how the reader responds to them. Louie is a reader herself and tries to interest Glenda in keeping in touch by leaving letters inside a book in what she jokingly calls the 'liberry'. Louie's Gran used to be a cleaner and remembers what else was left in books:

> 'They found a kipper bone in one, and a rasher of streaky bacon inside *Wolff's Anatomy for Artists*. I remember that particularly. It matched the pictures.'
> 'You wouldn't catch anyone doing that these days,' said Mum. 'Bacon's that dear it would be cheaper to leave money.'
> 'It would be cheaper to eat books,' said Gran.
> Louie imagined a paperback lying like a slice of bread in the frying pan, between two tomato halves and an egg. The

31

fat began to bubble. The book sizzled. Its pages opened and closed a few times, then turned brown and curled up crisply along the edges. Fried book: she could almost taste it.

The writer's imagination is conveying surrealist pictures to the mind of the reader who is learning with every page what words can do.

Glenda, of course, ignores Louie's idea but Louie finds a new friend and her 'dead letter' project results in a crowd of children pushing into the library.

'Traffic jam,' Jane said, 'and here comes the traffic warden. Scarper.'

Louie turned back for a moment to look down into the children's library. She could not see the floor. The room was full of heads, seething like fruit in a saucepan, at a rolling boil.

'No,' she said, 'not traffic jam; liberry jam,' and they went out, down the steps, three times round the liberry bush for luck, and into the car park.

In this story Jan Mark is using a generous vocabulary of words to do more than just record the action of the plot: she is persuading the reader that you can enjoy the sound of the words in your head while you read (you don't need someone else to read aloud to hear this) and feel the rhythm of her final sentences.

Jan Mark says of her writing:

I write about children because I like to have my characters in decent perspective, but I don't mind who reads the books. If I know that the book or story is *intended* for a child reader-ship and, in the case of the Antelopes, for children of a specific age, then it is only fair to construct the thing from a child's eye level. It is perfectly possible to write about children for adults but that involves an adult view of childhood. If the readers are expected to be children it is *their* viewpoint that ought to inform the story. Children who appear in adult stories are there for a purpose. Adults appear in children's stories because almost everything a child does is in some way influenced by adults. Trying to understand the way children think isn't the same as claiming to know what they want.

Some of my books obviously appeal to younger children, others seem to have found an adult readership, and, in a way, this is a safeguard. Since I do not know my audience in advance, I cannot aim at it. I can only try to write as well as I am able and hope to find a sympathetic response in anyone, of any age, who reads what I have written. I write to meet the demands of myself as an adult, not those of the child I once was.

Anyone who claims to know what children want is implying a homogeneity which does not exist. This is the language of mass advertising, which has no place in the writing of fiction, for children or anyone else.[11]

Here Jan Mark is explaining another of the paradoxes of writing (and publishing) for children: in writing about children she is not assuming that her readers will necessarily *be* children, even though she is willing to 'target' that audience when asked – to use the jargon of the all-important marketing people who must try to bring the books within reach of their most likely readers. If you look at one of her short stories, 'William's Version' from *Nothing to be Afraid Of*, you will see exactly what she means. William, who cannot yet read, is putting his grandmother right about the story of the three little pigs:

'The little pig put the saucepan on the gas stove and the wolf got down the chimney and put the little pig in the saucepan and boiled him. He had him for tea, with chips,' said William.

'Oh,' said Granny. 'I've got it all wrong, haven't I? Can I see the book, then I shall know, next time.'

William took the book from under his pullover. Granny opened it and read, *First Aid for Beginners: a Practical Handbook*.

'I see,' said Granny. 'I don't think I can read this. I left my glasses at home. You tell Gran how it ends.'

William turned to the last page which showed a prostrate man with his leg in a splint; *compound fracture of the femur*.

'Then the wolf washed up and got on his tricycle and went to see his Granny, and his Granny opened the door and said, "Hello, William".'

This is a story that makes adults laugh, in the same way that they laugh at short stories told with the wit of Alan Coren or Stephen

[11] *Twentieth-Century Children's Writers*

Leacock. An adult recognises at once the humour of the situation, which lies in the fact that William is asserting the right to *his* version of the story because he wants to make his mark with Granny. And he is anxious to do this because he suspects he will very soon have to move over and make room in her affection for a new baby. None of this is stated explicitly, of course; only the first sentence explains that William and Granny are entertaining each other while his mother goes to the clinic.

This kind of humour involves the writer in observing the situation from the outside, presenting William's viewpoint not directly but in what he does or says. It is all the more surprising to discover that children at the top end of the primary school, having passed beyond the early stages of learning to read, can appreciate this story and have learnt to 'read between the lines' without, apparently, ever having been taught how to do it. Margaret Meek, a specialist in children's reading, tells us this. She describes the process in *How Texts Teach What Readers Learn*, a booklet written primarily for teachers but of great help to any writer who wants to know more about children's responses to what they read.

This advance in reading skill represents the change in readership from 'younger' to 'older' children, although everyone, as we know, reads at different levels at different times. In publishing terms, as a convenient guide to customers, the division is set around a reading age of nine. For the writer, it means that different assumptions can be made about what young readers can tackle.

4. Writing for Older Children and Teenagers

As readers acquire increasing confidence and become more fluent, so their appetites grow for more and more stories of all kinds – adventure, family, fantasy, historical, mystery, school, thriller – and you can assume that the range of subject-matter you can consider is almost limitless. You are certainly not confined to what lies within a child's own experience, and when thinking about an idea that has come into your mind you can rely on common sense to decide whether it's a story to be written for children or adults. A mystery about insider dealing on the stock exchange might not interest children; a robbery in which children played a part in catching the criminals might make a cops-and-robbers story for them (and often has). A story in which a child was the thief, got away with it and showed no remorse – ah, there's the catch. *That*, I think, could only be told as a psychological thriller for adults. For most people would agree, I believe, that in a story for children justice should be seen to be done, and the challenge for the writer is to admit, and gradually introduce into realistic stories, the possibility that *in*justice, evil, wickedness – however you name it, whatever its origin – exists in similar measure to its opposite.

At the picture-book stage parents (whether two or one, together or separated) are invariably caring and protective; children may be naughty but are forgiven; danger lies in natural but minor disasters (things lost, but found again; things broken, but mended or replaced). In fairy stories, the wicked are wicked all through and get their deserts, while the frog is turned back into a prince. In fantasies for the very young, robbers and pirates are caught and made to walk the plank, or sometimes become Reformed Characters.

But as children's knowledge of the world deepens, so there has to come into stories the recognition that parents can sometimes tell lies, run away, that friends can let you down, that you are on your own in an adult world, which can often look very bleak.

Betsy Byars, an American, writes about children in realistic, often daunting situations. Her books are very funny (a good way of meeting this challenge), and she writes in a direct, economical style that suits her unsentimental view of childhood. When she starts a book, she says, she doesn't usually know which way the characters will take her. 'The story grows as I write, and I have never done a book that didn't take some surprising turn as the story developed.'

One of her most popular books, *The Eighteenth Emergency*:

> ... began in my girlhood. I went to a country school, and the terrors of the school were the Fletcher brothers. Everyone – including the teachers and the principal – was terrified of them. I can't remember anything that the Fletcher brothers actually did, but the thought of what they might do kept me awake at night. Later I consolidated the Fletcher brothers into the dreaded Marv Hammerman of *The Eighteenth Emergency*. Actually I wanted to call the bully Fletcher, but those Fletcher boys are still out there somewhere.[1]

Mouse is the boy who writes the dreaded Hammerman's name on a chart in the school history room, with an arrow pointing to Neanderthal man. As he thinks about what Hammerman will do to him, his mother makes the standard adult response, 'In a few weeks you'll look back on this and laugh', but of course Mouse knows this can't be true. He and his friend Ezzie had once worked out seventeen ways to meet any jungle emergency ('When attacked by a crocodile, prop a stick in its mouth and the crocodile is helpless') but to the eighteenth emergency of a fight with Hammerman, Mouse can see no solution:

> It seemed to him suddenly that what most emergency measures amounted to was doing whatever was most unnatural. If it was natural to start screaming, survival called for keeping perfectly quiet. If it was natural to run, the best thing to do was to stand still. Whatever was the hardest, that was what you had to do sometimes to survive. The hardest thing of all, it seemed to him, was not running.

[1]'Oak Leaves and Spider Webs and other debts of gratitude', Proceedings of the Second Pacific Rim Conference on Children's Literature, 1980

When, after Mouse has been thoroughly bruised by Hammerman, he has not gone down, has not cried, he can hardly believe he is still the same person:

> ... for the first time he knew what real relief was. It was a relief so great that the whole world looked different to him, cleaner and sharper. He had not even felt this way when he got out of the hospital after losing his tonsils. It was the kind of light feeling that might come with a lessening of the pull of gravity. He felt that if he wanted to, he could actually float up through the buildings. He imagined himself rising, moving slowly and easily, waving to the startled people in the windows, smiling to them. His body was the lightest, most unburdened thing in the world. Strings would be required in a minute to hold him to the ground.

You can see what is happening here: any reader who has feared something terrible and watched it pass will recognise what Mouse feels like and identify with him. It doesn't matter what age or gender you are, Mouse's feeling of lightness and elation is yours. I think the lesson that can be learnt from Betsy Byars' writing is that, as well as knowing your child characters inside out, you really have to like them, to the extent that you can imagine easily how they are thinking and what they are feeling. 'I have come to see,' says Betsy, 'that children do not think like adults, act like adults, or talk like adults. And even though we adults sometimes feel that we are exactly the same as when we were ten, I think that's because we can no longer conceive of what ten was really like, and because what we have lost, we have lost so gradually that we no longer miss it.'

Taking the child's viewpoint

Although you can now assume that your readers can take any number of technical hurdles in their stride – changes of tense, changes of place and leaps in time from chapter to chapter, things left unsaid (teachers tell us children can 'fill in the gaps' at an early age) – the point of view from which the story is told becomes even more important.

This is well demonstrated in a novel by Philippa Pearce whose plot could be thought most appropriate to an adult detective thriller or an adult novel of intense family relationships. *The Way to Sattin Shore* is about two brothers. After a violent quarrel, they make up and go for a moonlight swim in a river estuary. One gets into difficulties and the other drags him ashore, leaving him unconscious while fetching help. But he dies, for the survivor had forgotten the incoming tide – or had he? Exonerated by the coroner, this brother nevertheless runs away in panic, while his wife gives birth to their third child and her mother determines they will tell the children he is dead. Ten years later the runaway returns, and his children break down the barriers of silence and bitterness that have kept his existence hidden.

Now see what Philippa Pearce does with this plot. Her novel, about 50,000 words in length, is divided into fairly short chapters. Each is headed with a descriptive title and a small line drawing that is not so much an illustration, more a decorative breathing space. The focus, from the start, is on the child born at the time of the tragedy: a girl whose physical appearance is never described, whose age is never mentioned (though you learn early on that *she* understands she was born the day her father died, ten years before), but whom you soon feel you know well simply because you see everything through her eyes, learn what she discovers, feel what she feels.

The first words read almost like an announcement, a stage direction, a helpful introduction:

> Here is Kate Tranter coming home from school in the January dusk – the first to come, because she is the youngest of her family. Past the churchyard. Past the shops. Along the fronts of the tall, narrow terrace houses she goes. Not this one, nor this one, nor this …
> Stop at the house with no lit window.
> This is home.

Then a shift of the focus:

> Up three steps to the front door, and feel for the key on the string in her pocket. Unlock, and then in.

Only now does the narrative move into the past tense, and as the narrator's voice disappears the reader is inside Kate Tranter, going through the house, past Granny's room, realising it's Granny who lives in the dark ('no lit window'), up the stairs, into Kate's bedroom where her cat Syrup is waiting for her. Then the reader is listening, with Kate, to the sounds of the house, the happenings at the end of the school day – concentration is on the details of the moment, the preoccupation of a child with the present.

It sounds very obvious, but a mistake that's made so often is to spell out every move. You don't need to write, in fact you ruin the illusion if you write (and of course this author doesn't), '*Kate noticed* that her grandmother's door was open. *Kate felt...*' Your reader should already be inside Kate's mind, so that what Kate notices is what the reader sees through your words. You step over the threshold of Kate's house so that you are writing the story from the inside rather than the outside. So your reader can literally be any age but while inside the story becomes the age of Kate.

Still in the first chapter, the mystery begins. As Kate takes the tea tray into her grandmother's room, she hears footsteps coming to the front door. A letter with no stamp is pushed through the letterbox, a car drives away. The letter is addressed to the grandmother, who shouts for her daughter as she opens it. While the children are eating their tea, nothing is said. It is obvious that their mother is often silent, that the children accept this and don't ask questions.

But the next day Kate tries to ask her elder brother Randall about it.

'Well?' he said at the end.

'Well, don't you think it was funny – I mean, odd – what happened?'

'I don't think it was odd or not odd. It's just none of our business.'

'But it's our grandmother, and it happened in our house!'

'Not our house; her house.'

Kate responds by bursting into tears, but the reader now, by Chapter 2, has two questions niggling in the back of the mind. What was in that letter? Why does the Tranters' home belong to their grandmother?

The third chapter brings another hint – hardly a clue – of something strange and wrong. Kate's two brothers are squabbling; their squabble becomes a fight.

Lenny and Ran stopped fighting, but their mother had seen them. 'Why do you two have to quarrel?' she demanded. She spoke with the ordinary, commonplace little despair of fed-upness; her question did not expect an answer.

But, from behind her, came old Mrs Randall's voice, as if she were talking only to herself, yet distinctly: 'Quarrelling – fighting: they inherit it ...'

Kate saw her mother's face change, whiten. She was staring at the two boys as if she saw them quite differently; or perhaps she saw quite different boys.

And here the 'Kate saw' is necessary, if only to heighten the drama of the moment – it's something she has never seen, or perhaps never realised, before.

Whereas, in an adult novel, the mystery would have remained at the forefront of the story, here the moment passes, nothing more is said about the quarrel, and the mystery is forgotten in the preoccupation of Kate and her brother Lenny with the snow that, to their relief, lasts until the weekend when they go sliding and tobogganing. Nothing matters but the exhilarating excitement of that day in the snow.

With the thaw comes the need to put away the toboggan in the loft, and when the friend who does this returns, he says,

> 'There's a camp-bed, in a plastic bag. Rolls of wallpaper in a suitcase. There are some pillows, too. Would those all be your mum's?'
> 'Of course.'
> 'I just wondered ...' For a moment Kate thought that Brian was going to say more; but he changed his mind. 'I just wondered,' he repeated.

Another part of the jigsaw: in one of the pillows the grand-mother has hoarded money with which, finally, she hopes to bribe the son-in-law not to return.

There has been no mention so far of Kate ever thinking about her father, though she visits what she believes is his grave. ('No one knew that she knew exactly where to find her father's grave. She had found it by accident over a year ago.') But now her friend, Anna, whose parents are divorcing, has an idea.

> Anna said: 'Your mum's a widow, isn't she?'
> 'Yes,' said Kate, a step behind Anna in her thinking.
> 'Well,' said Anna, 'when my dad's got his divorce, he could

40

marry your mum.' ... Kate was bewildered by the suddenness of the project.

'But – I mean, I don't think my mum wants to marry anyone.'

And Kate feels uneasy – as does the reader – until the subject is forgotten in another excitement of the moment, the making of pancakes.

As the mystery is slowly unravelled, it is always Kate's viewpoint that dictates what the reader sees, what the reader knows. Much is left unsaid; the pauses at the end of chapters give time to put the pieces of the jigsaw together. The house that in an adult novel might have been filled with the bitter atmosphere of the unforgiving grandmother and the mother who's been deserted is accepted without question as home by the child who loves her attic bedroom where Syrup her cat sleeps on her bed. The pieces of the mystery that uncover the darkness of what happened before her birth are interspersed with the happiness of everyday events in which she is totally absorbed.

What in a novel for adults might have turned into a study of mother-daughter relationships becomes a quest for a father that at times overwhelms Kate's dreams, both awake and asleep; yet in between she can be totally absorbed in her everyday activities, an absorption the reader shares. We have only glimpses of what her mother is feeling and doing, for to Kate she is simply an immovable part of the secure haven of home, and she says no more than Kate needs to hear.

And since this is Kate's story, and a story for children, the scene of reconciliation between runaway husband and wife takes place offstage – Kate isn't interested in the how or why, she just sees what she sees:

> And there was her mother, Kitty Tranter, with her changed face, too: not happier or sadder, not more loving – or more hating. None of those things, or other things that Kate might have expected. Just changed utterly in expression, changed into something new and strange.

The ends are tied up. There's no hiding of the fact that the grandmother will never forgive the son-in-law, but she can be safely left behind when the family start afresh in Australia. There is no speculation about how the ten-year absence will be made up, or why the brothers quarrelled, or how the older ones will adjust to the new situation. The ending is more robust: Kate, having found a father and knowing that her two grand-mothers are looked after and her cat gratefully left with one of them, is happy. 'Deeply, dreamlessly, she slept.'

If you compare Philippa Pearce's novel with Susan Hill's *I'm the King of the Castle* or Elizabeth Bowen's *The House in Paris* – in both of which children play a major part – you will see the difference between writing for adults and writing for children.

Fantasy

The two children's books I have just described are both realistic stories, but their settings – an American small town and an English market town – will not represent the background of all their readers, however much those readers may identify with the protagonists. Both authors are thoroughly familiar with those settings, and it is obviously best, if you can, to set your story in a place you know well. But for many writers fantasy, in which the setting can be partly or entirely an imaginary world, seems the ideal way of telling a story for children. This genre certainly gives you freedom, in that you don't have to do any research, as you would if you were setting your story in another time or in a place you had not seen. On the other hand, you have to remember that an imaginary setting must be both convincing and *inviting* – whether for the thrill of being frightened by the horror of the place or the comfort of escaping from your usual surroundings to somewhere more congenial. To make the other world convincing, you may have to spend a lot of effort thinking about much more than its superficial appearance, for even though it may be a nonsensical world (topsy-turvy, for instance) its features must follow some consistent pattern, or the reader will not take it seriously. (Look at the care with which Mary Norton created the world of *The Borrowers*, where even their names are borrowed.)

Yet the setting should not take over completely. Fantasy seems to inspire people to write at length, and I have often regretted having to reject manuscripts that had obviously been prepared in much painstaking detail. The trouble seemed to be that the writer had become so preoccupied with this other world that all the creative energy had gone into its loving construction, with not much thought left for the purpose of it all. As ever, the story is of prime importance and the setting, however intriguing, is not enough to sustain a poor story line.

A first novel that seemed to me to avoid the pitfalls of the genre – and won the Smarties Prize in 1990 – was *Midnight Blue* by Pauline Fisk. In this story the fantasy is only fractionally removed from reality and it originates in the heroine's dreams of what she imagines might constitute happiness, for life so far has not treated her very well. Her mother is inadequate, her father is never mentioned; her grandmother appears to her a dominating and cruel figure, despising her daughter and convinced that she alone can bring up her granddaughter properly.

Bonnie runs away from her inner-city flat to a rural farmhouse where she finds herself, her mother and her missing father mirrored in characters who make up a loving family. Alongside these 'dream' people are mythical characters representing the traditional elements of good and evil, but their part in the action is subsidiary to the main theme. Even the running away, accomplished by a method of hot-air ballooning that seems magical, is – as the author explains in an end-note – perfectly possible.

Thus, in letting fantasy and reality overlap, the writer has turned the old clichés of the genre inside out. There is no symbolic battle between opposing forces of the good and the bad, but moving between real family and dream family the heroine learns that what she sees as hatred between mother and grandmother may be lack of trust, and that where there is love envy has no place.

I used to worry a lot about the dividing line in children's fiction between what could really happen and what could not – and whether this should be explained – until I learned that children have no such problems in making the distinction between fact and imagination. J.R.R. Tolkien, who created in *The Hobbit* a fantasy world with even a language of its own, once wrote of his love of dragons as a child:

I never imagined that the dragon was of the same order as the horse. And that was not solely because I saw horses daily, but never even the footprint of a worm ...

Of course, I in my timid body did not wish to have them in the neighbourhood, intruding into my relatively safe world, in which it was, for instance, possible to read stories in peace of mind, free from fear ...

This is, naturally, often enough what children mean when they ask 'Is it true?' They mean: 'I like this, but is it contemporary? Am I safe in my bed?' The answer: 'There is certainly no dragon in England today' is all that they want to hear.[2]

Though this was written half a century ago, I am sure it remains true, as experienced writers know. Roald Dahl, that phenomenon among storytellers, can even play with his readers, knowing that they will see the joke, when in *The Witches* he describes the stories told to him by his grandmother.

> 'Are you *really* being truthful, Grandmamma? *Really* and *truly* truthful?'
> 'My darling,' she said, 'you won't last long in this world if you don't know how to spot a witch when you see one.'

Roald Dahl's voice is so distinctive and so familiar to his readers that they know exactly what he means – even as he says of the stories 'They were the *gospel* truth', they know it's just an amazing idea, and 'what fun and excitement' to believe it!

So, you can set fantastic characters in a background of reality, transfer real characters to a landscape of fantasy, if this is what your story demands, and your readers will have no difficulty in accepting it. Sometimes you can say much more about a larger-than-life character: compare the bully, Marv Hammerman, in *The Eighteenth Emergency* with his counterpart, Elvis Cave, in Philip Ridley's fantasy *Krindlekrax*. Hammerman is scarcely articulate; like the original Fletcher brothers who inspired him, it's the thought of what he *might* do that gives him any sort of substance. But Elvis, though only a nine-year-old boy, has grown so tall and so strong that when he walks down the street in his sleep he breaks every window with his bouncing football, terrorising everyone. And when he gets his comeuppance the broad humour with which the story is told allows him to break down in tears, admitting that all he ever wanted was to be liked.

Fantasy gives you scope for caricature, which is perhaps as close to satire as you can get in writing for children. Irony, yes;

[2] 'On Fairy-Stories', *Essays Presented to Charles Williams*, 1947

readers quite swiftly get the hang of humour that depends on words being used to imply the opposite of what they usually mean. But satire, which depends on an understanding of the human failings or aspects of society being held up to ridicule, is maybe best appreciated by teenage or adult readers. Unless, of course, you regard Roald Dahl's stories for children as satirical, for they are enormously popular with children under ten, but to my mind his ridiculing of adults is simply a tremendous joke seen from the children's viewpoint. Despite his great success, it would be a mistake to use him as a role model for, with a life-time of writing experience, he could push the boundaries of adult sensibilities to the limit and get away with it, as no newcomer could. It is a pity, I think, that the judges who gave the Whitbread Award[3] for 1983 to *The Witches* are quoted as saying, 'Funny, wise, deliciously disgusting, a *real* book for children', which is a bit like saying, 'Funny, wise, deliciously sexy, a *real* book for adults'. But there you are again – if you want to write children's books, even if you are in the prize-winning class, be prepared to be patronised.

The writing of historical fiction has been so well covered by Rhona Martin in another book in this series that I cannot add anything to her advice, except to recommend that, if you are interested in writing a historical novel for children, you should read the two other books shortlisted for the Whitbread Award in 1983, *The Donkey's Crusade* by Jean Morris, and *A Parcel of Patterns* by Jill Paton Walsh.

Teenage novels

There is continual argument about whether novels specially written and published for teenagers are actually read by adolescents, who (it is said) either move on quite happily to adult novels or stop reading for pleasure altogether as soon as they step on to the school examination treadmill. In my opinion there is no doubt that certain books, whether specially written with them in

---

[3]This annual award, first made in 1972, originally offered £2,000 to the winner in each of five categories, with an overall prize of £20,500. The latter was never won by a children's novel, and in 1996 a new award, the Whitbread Children's Book of the Year, worth £10,000, replaced the children's category

mind or not, have a particular appeal to teenage readers, and it is the responsibility of publishers to produce those books in such a way that their potential readers can find them easily.

The development of this branch of publishing dates back to the late 1960s, when Aidan Chambers (a writer himself, and then teaching in a secondary school for eleven- to sixteen-year-olds) in a book entitled *The Reluctant Reader* argued the case for separately published fiction for the readers he was teaching. Almost simultaneously, two novels that appeared on children's lists uncovered the hidden barriers that stood between the teenage novel and its readers.

The first, Alan Garner's *The Owl Service*, is a novel about two adolescent boys and a girl, whose story is interwoven with another of a previous generation and a legend from the Welsh *Mabinogion*. Alan Garner, who has described his prose as 'long narrative poetry', has said that he writes with no specific sense of his audience – it is the story in his head that dictates the form it will take. The heroine of the Welsh legend is a woman made out of flowers, and the final paragraph of the book will give you some idea of the feel of the prose and the atmosphere of the novel:

> And the room was full of petals from skylight and rafters, and all about them a fragrance, and petals, flowers falling, broom, meadowsweet, falling, flowers of the oak.

The novel won the Carnegie Medal for 1967 as well as the *Guardian* award.[4] Among its many admiring reviews, one appeared by chance on the adult books page of *The Sunday Times*. This resulted in a request for the book in a public library, which caused complete bewilderment until it was realised that *The Owl Service* would have been categorised in BNB (the British National Bibliography published weekly by the British Library) as J for Juvenile, and therefore not even to be considered for purchase by a library serving readers over the age of fourteen. In those days the division between children's and adult libraries was so wide that transferring from one to the other amounted almost to a ceremony of initiation, and it was not surprising to find that many children drifted away from the

[4]An annual award for a children's novel, now worth £1,500

library long before they could make the change. And yet the readers for *The Owl Service* were in that very age band that should have spanned the two.

While Alan Garner had already written three books for children, the American Paul Zindel was a playwright and had never thought of writing a novel until an editor in New York (where the Young Adult novel was an established genre) suggested the idea to him. His response was to ask the kids who were learning chemistry with him. What was a YA novel?

> They said they hadn't read any. They read comics, they saw movies, they didn't read books. But if they had read a novel, it was *Catcher in the Rye*, because their girlfriends made them read it. So I looked at the book again and I realised what the author had done. He spoke like kids think, and he spoke closest to the way that kids spoke in the school where I taught. And after that I just responded to those things I saw in the kids I taught that reflected the world as I saw it.[5]

Although Paul Zindel claims that all he had to do was put down all the strange things he'd done and observed in High School, and to do this in the way the kids talked, there was of course more to it. He gave the narrative in *The Pigman* to two characters, a girl and a boy, talking in turn with two points of view, and interspersed the text with handwritten messages and diagrams to add authenticity to the teenage voices. The result was very different from anything written in the English literary tradition. This you can see in the ending. The plot, a tragic one, concerns a group of teenagers who play the telephone game and meet a lonely, eccentric old man. ('We made up a new game in which the object was to keep a stranger talking on the telephone for as long as possible ...') Without realising what they are doing, the teenagers wreck his home and indirectly cause his death.

> We had trespassed too – been where we didn't belong, and we were being punished for it. Mr Pignati had paid with his life. But when he died something in us had died as well.
> There was no one else to blame any more ...

[5] Authorgraph No. 54, *Books for Keeps*, January 1989

Our life would be what we made of it – nothing more, nothing less.

Baboons.

Baboons.

They build their own cages, we could almost hear the Pigman whisper, as he took his children with him.

Here was clearly a new voice. Faced with the dilemma of how to present *The Pigman* in 1969 – when library users were so firmly divided into what Hugh Lofting called 'Juveniles' and 'Seniles' – the British publisher decided simply to label it 'A Book for New Adults', as a signal to those on the receiving end that this novel could not be segregated in either category. The label (using the term by which the government addressed the newly enfranchised eighteen-year-olds) was not needed for long; it drew attention to a situation that quickly improved. In the following decade the library barrier disappeared.

Meanwhile publishers began to identify teenage novels either by a distinctive style of production (photographic covers, for instance, were then something new), a series name (Puffin Plus, Collins' Teen Tracks, Corgi's Freeway, Deutsch's Adlibs), or a growing backlist of books by a recognised writer of this type of story (John Rowe Townsend, Jill Paton Walsh, for instance). The style of the British writers remained distinct from that of the Americans, which was much closer to the spoken language and seemed to many teachers to give them the edge in communicating with their teenage audience. But the American novels concentrated so firmly on the difficulties of growing up that in the 1970s and early 1980s no problem could apparently be left untouched. Problems seem now to have been set aside in favour of issues, but teenage fiction does appear to be influenced more than other parts of publishing by 'trends'.

Approaches

For the writer today who is interested in writing for this age group I think there are three ways of approach. First – as with all kinds of fiction – an idea may come to you with such force that you will write about it, come hell or high water, whatever anyone may tell you about its chances of publication. Ideas sometimes start with people, or with situations; they may come from incidents of your own adolescence; they may arise from something you have read. If the idea is appropriate to adolescence, then the chances are that the story will shape itself in your mind from that viewpoint.

Second, you can go out and observe young people, ask what concerns them, find out how they are thinking, and if this sparks off an idea, you may end up with a novel like *The Pigman* (still in print after over twenty-five years). But Zindel was careful to remember:

> If I had tried to write exactly as the teenagers spoke, it would have dated immediately. So I knew I didn't want to do that. I speak usually in two ways: I speak in hyperbole, and I speak in bathos. I tend to take either the common object and refer to it in a way that connects it to something elevated, or I take a very high concept and combine it with a very down-to-earth term. It gives the *illusion* of slang and it gives the illusion of surprise.

So if you write a realistic novel, you must find your own style and voice.

And third, you can practise your skill as a writer in following a pattern devised by someone else for a series. The books that sell directly in vast quantities to the sub-teen readers are (we are told) American paperback series like the Babysitters Club (stories about the same seven familiar characters), Goosebumps, Sweet Valley High, and Point Horror (stories that chill and thrill, with strongly defined good and bad characters). So far, British publishers have had limited success in trying to emulate this form of publishing, but if, after looking at examples of the American series, you think you could write to a formula, send a sample of your writing to a publisher who has such a series.

Books of this last kind are not highly regarded by adults, but perhaps young readers are able to distinguish between different types of fiction just as well as their elders. In the adult field pulp fiction is recognised as ephemeral entertainment, quickly read and as easily forgotten. With children and teenagers, their pulp fiction tends to be defined as what they shouldn't read but do, and literary fiction as what we'd like them to read but they don't. Surely everyone reads different kinds of book according to need, taste or occasion – but children sometimes need a helper to guide them into trying something new.

First-person narrative

In whatever way you approach the teenage novel, you will find it vital to do some research into current teenage behaviour, to ensure that the way your characters think and speak is convincing and not spoilt by anachronistic detail. You may want to write in the first person, because this type of narration offers what looks like an easy method of getting inside the main character and of giving extra emphasis to the emotional content of the story that now becomes so important. Although this is effective when it works well, there are pitfalls. First, there is the obvious snag that the narrator can't be everywhere at once and some incidents have to be told at second-hand – and this can become clumsy. Second, as Zindel pointed out, if you try to reproduce exactly the way the narrator might really write or speak, the use of transitory language – slang or jargon – may make the text less convincing because it sounds dated. Third, some writers believe the narrative is equally unconvincing unless there is some good reason for one of the characters to be telling the story. Nadia Wheatley, the Australian author of *The Blooding*, feels strongly about this.

> What annoys me about a lot of these novels is that it is not often explained *why* the character writes. I couldn't do that. I had to have an explanation and then I had the problem of how Col, a seventeen-year-old kid, had the ability to write. Lots of the narrators in these diary-novels report dialogue as though they have a perfect memory and perfect ear. I couldn't go along with that. I had to justify it. Col speaks to the reader to give himself a reason for saying some of the things he does. I *know* it was clumsy, but the point is that Col was a clumsy writer. Also, he was lonely, and he wanted someone to talk to![6]

So the first sentence of the novel reads:

The Lawyer said to write down what happened.

The use of that colloquial phrase 'said to' makes it immediately clear that the narrator is using a speaking rather than a writing

---

[6]*No Kidding: Top Writers for Young People Talk about Their Work*, Agnes Nieuwenhuizen, 1991

voice – and frequently in his recording of what happened, Col interrupts himself to explain what he is doing.

> When I read yesterday's bit, I saw how I'm kind of explaining everything to someone called 'you'.
> So HI! there, whoever you are! Here we go again.

Here the writer is taking risks, in almost daring the reader to stop listening, but if by this time the reader is truly concerned about the narrator, wants to know more about him, then it *is*, almost paradoxically, a way of adding authenticity to what he is telling. Nadia Wheatley's hero is writing from a hospital bed, so she obviously had to find another way of telling what is happening now, outside. Newspaper reports delivered to her hero fit this role exactly – for her plot involves a political scandal about the logging business on which a local community depends for its economy and against which the 'greenies' are protesting by sitting in the trees.

A novel that makes dramatic use of two first-person narratives is *Dear Nobody* by Berlie Doherty, which is also notable as the winner of the Carnegie Medal for 1991. The award, to an outstanding book *for children*, is made as a result of nominations from librarians working with children throughout the UK. Since *Dear Nobody* is about a teenage pregnancy (the girl is eighteen), this choice was significant in giving recognition to a teenage novel that the librarians plainly considered within the imaginative grasp of a twelve-year-old, although the story is told rather differently from either a children's book or an adult novel.

This is partly to do with the two narrators: Chris, who records the story looking back from the day the baby is born to the day it was conceived, and Helen, who writes letters to her unborn child and sends them all to Chris just hours before the baby's birth. Both Chris and Helen are in their last year at school, both expected to do well in their A-levels. In dividing the narrative between them, Berlie Doherty has not attempted to give either any obtrusive distinguishing marks in style, nor has she made them use any teenage slang. (They talk about each other in tender, almost delicate language.) Yet their voices are quite recognisable, while every so often each narrative drifts into dialogue that makes the reader temporarily forget there is no third 'author' narrator. Chris's best subject is English, so it's not unlikely he could write a story like this, but it's as a person, rather than a storyteller, that he is convincing, from the very beginning:

> Maybe we all want to burn off across the horizon, into space, perhaps, to take off into some unknown territory and meet ourselves out there. This book is a kind of journey, but I don't know yet where it's all going to end.
>
> It all began last January, on a dark evening that was full of sleet. Funny, it's not long ago. I was just a kid then. But today is October 2nd, and this is where I begin to write, where I open a door into the past.

The first sentence, with its contemporary phrase 'burn off', signals that the narrator is young, perhaps not of an age to be the author. 'It all began ...' could have been a cliché, but here the date is all-important – as you realise as soon as you see that the story is broken into the sections of the nine months following. The tone of the writing is disarming: here is someone going to be open with you, to tell you honestly what's happened. How can you not believe him?

This, I think, is the clue to both the attraction of the first-person narrative and the particular success of *Dear Nobody*. Chris writes entirely without guile; Helen hides nothing from her unborn child. The reader warms to them instinctively and begins almost at once to care about what will happen to them. How does Berlie Doherty make this work? For a start, she obviously has great affection for her two main characters. Whether she modelled them on real people I do not know, but her dedication says:

> While I was writing this book I talked to many young people. *Dear Nobody* is for all of them.

Secondly, she passes no judgement. It is clear from one discreet sentence on the first page that the boy and girl made love for the first time in a moment of supreme happiness. They are both very frightened by the pregnancy but there is no evasion of responsibility, no railing against fate. Helen is brave, resourceful, and she sits her A-levels without problem. But it is her attitude towards her baby, 'Nobody', that keeps the reader in thrall – treating it as a person with a generosity that is characteristic of the young and the exact opposite of the way Helen's own mother retreats into tight-lipped bitterness and her grandmother slips away from reality into everlasting daydreams.

What separates this book from the children's category of story – apart from the subject matter, although there are no references to sex that could be found objectionable – is that, while the story is told from the viewpoints of Chris and Helen, the reader is made aware of the wider implications of the situation, which are revealed through what parents say, what parents don't say. Chris, in interpreting what others are saying and feeling, shows that he is more adult than child.

Why this book was not published as an adult novel is that the focus is firmly on the emotional relationship between Helen and Chris and how two teenagers face a crisis of adult responsibility. In an adult novel Chris's final words might be found suspect, as unrealistically romantic; the writer would have implied, somehow, that life for Amy may be tough. In a teenage novel, the words of Chris, who does not know what is ahead, ring true:

> So, in my student's room in Newcastle, I'm writing this for you, Amy. Your name means loved one, or friend, and we both chose it. This is your story, and you should know it. One day a long time from now you will read it and put together all the bits and pieces of people that have gone together to make you.

Berlie Doherty has written for both children and adults. She says of this book:

> To have a novel on a teenage list can be a dangerous thing – I know too well how some of the most avid readers leap from reading children's fiction into reading books for adults, and never seek out that half-way shelf. I think it's a shame when that happens. Teenagers, of all people, need to find themselves in the literature that they read, and to explore the whirlpool of conflicting emotions into which they have been flung.
>
> I knew that in *Dear Nobody* I was handling a difficult situation. The challenge I set myself was to write a novel about teenage love that was not a piece of romance fiction ...

If you want to write for teenagers, you may find it difficult to get your first story published, for – in this area of publishing more than any other – establishing the initial link between writer and reader is the publisher's greatest problem, as I hope I have explained. But, as Aidan Chambers has said:

> Young adult literature is not, to my mind, a ghetto intended for and restricted to those who live in that patch. Nor is it a genre,

for it includes work in many genres, such as detective stories and science fiction, romances whether of the sentimental or the fantastic kind, naturalistic novels about contemporary life, and so on. No, the features that set it apart are that its central concern is the adolescent experience, and that its depiction of adolescence becomes an image for, a metaphor of, the whole of life. The result should be a book in which both adolescent and adult readers mutually find significant meaning for their own, individual lives.[7]

Translations

The traffic in translations has, until recently, been mainly one way, British children's books being translated into Danish, Dutch, French, German, Swedish and so on. Perhaps the breaking down of barriers within the EU will mean more books coming the other way.

If you want to offer your services as a translator, the best way of setting about it is to send a sample of your writing to publishers with a note of the languages in which you are fluent. The quality of your writing style is as important as your knowledge of the language concerned. If you find a book in another language that you think suitable for translation, remember that it will be the original publisher who controls the right to license an English edition – so don't spend too much time on a sample translation, in case the book has already been sold to a London publisher. A few sample pages, together with a summary of the book's contents, will be enough for a publisher to make a decision whether to acquire the book.

Good translators, who can produce an English text that reads fluently to children and yet retains something of the strangeness of the original, are rare. So, if you have that skill, it is certainly worth cultivating. You can also make a start by offering to read and report on children's books in foreign languages, although the fees for such work are not usually high.

[7] 'All of a Tremble to See His Danger', May Hill Arbuthnot Honor Lecture, 1986

5. Writing Non-Fiction

Curiosity is a strong motivator. If children want information and it can be found in a book, then they will not be deterred by what looks like a complex piece of writing, even a book written with adults in mind. Similarly, adult readers often find a book intended for children closer to their comprehension because of its lucid presentation of a subject. In this area of children's books, therefore, the reading experience of the audience is not as important as the writer's understanding of how children learn, what knowledge young readers can be assumed to have already, and the methods of teaching currently in use. Although children's non-fiction books are conceived, written, published and marketed in a different way from school text books, they are widely used in schools and publishers employ advisers, or conduct research themselves, to keep up to date with the needs of teachers. (In the primary school, children's books are often kept in both a central library, or resource room, and in dispersed collections, each classroom having its own.)

If you want to write this kind of book, you need to have the skill of writing lucidly, thorough knowledge of your subject and experience of children learning. Conveying information is very different from writing fiction, where you are introducing your reader to characters in a situation you have created and about which they know nothing in advance. Jennifer Wilson, a teacher and regular assessor of children's information books, offers this advice:

> When children first become interested in information, it is not packaged in books. Curiosity about the natural world and their physical environment arises from direct contact with it and from conversation which directs and extends their observation and experimental approach.

By the time children make use of information books ... they have undertaken a good deal of research in many different contexts, from playing around in rockpools on holiday, helping with the cooking at home or finding out what will sink and float when so much water goes overboard that they almost become part of the experiment. One thing which is always greeted with enthusiasm at school is the practical lesson, whether its justification is history, geography or science.

It is, therefore, the pleasure of this first-hand experience which children bring to information books, and one way of building up criteria for choosing them may be to examine more closely what children's expectations are. They should find that books are as rigorous as they are in the exercise of natural curiosity in both structured and informal settings. Thus they will be 'listening' to make sure that all the senses are used in describing things and for the apt simile which brings word pictures into focus. They will be looking for evidence in the history they read; they can produce plenty for themselves to support their first-hand experience. They can recognise the difference between the intimate detail in which you talk about the place where you live and the patchy knowledge of a visitor, and they turn to books about other lands to 'live' there through the eyes of someone else, not to visit them via the scanty, selective information of a holiday brochure.[1]

Nor is any reader – of whatever age – likely to be excited by a book that begins:

Most tunnels are long holes dug underground. Very small tunnels are dug by ants and worms. They live in them.

or:

Any object flown in the air at the end of a line is called a kite.

By the time you can read sentences like this, you will surely have encountered ants, kites, tunnels *and* worms.

The range of books covered by the category 'non-fiction' is very large. It includes reference books (dictionaries, atlases, encyclopaedias), poetry (anthologies, poetry specially written for

[1]*The Signal Selection of Children's Books 1988*

56

children), music (song books), crafts (cooking, making puppets), handbooks (a guide to life as a teenage vegetarian, improving your baseball) and, much the biggest group, information books. (I have included poetry here, following the usual library classification.) 'Information' can cover every subject from biography to zoology, with emphasis now on books for 'home learning', produced with parents of preschool children in mind, and books for use in project work in school. Much of this publishing is done in series, partly for identification of subject matter and age level (Revolution! for readers in the secondary school; Bright Sparks, 'a general science series for seven and over') and partly to establish a uniform structure for the presentation of the material. Most of the books have a large element of illustration, of every kind. Photographs, artwork, collage, diagrams, cartoons, pictures created by computer technology – all are used, sometimes separately sometimes together, as a vital complement to the text.

Information books

If you look at some of the information books in your local library – where you will most likely find them arranged by subject, not by age level – you will probably see a list of people credited on the acknowledgements page, if not on the title-page, as contributors to its making. In a picture book of as few as twenty-four pages, for instance, you may read the names of the series or project editor, the art editor, the designer, the photographers (there is often more than one), the illustrator(s), and the picture researcher. The writer (whose name is probably on the title-page) must be ready to work as part of this team, who will together plan each page or double-spread, so that the information is presented as clearly as possible, illustrations and text integrated as closely as necessary. The proportion of text to pictures will vary from book to book. In some, the text may be only one sentence to a page, perhaps in the form of a question to stimulate the reader to think about what is shown in the picture. In others, the text may be of some length, with illustrations acting only as evidence of what has been described in words.

Most publishers prefer to commission books of non-fiction, having already conceived the idea of what they want, and having researched the market to find out what is needed. This does not mean that – if you have an idea for presenting in an original way a subject that interests you to the point of obsession – publishers would not be willing to consider it. The writers in short supply, and the writers publishers are always seeking, are those who can inspire readers with enthusiasm to find out more as well as satisfying curiosity with explanations that are accurate and easily understood. The writer of fiction has to seize hold of the reader with the very first sentence (what is going to happen next?), and the writer of non-fiction has to do the same (what makes this happen? why does it happen? how does it happen?). In writing non-fiction, where the reader is frequently addressed directly, it is important to remember how much has changed in the way people talk to children. Didacticism ('I am doing you good') was implicit in a great deal of writing for children, even in a series that seemed, nearly sixty years ago, far ahead of its time. Puffin Picture Books (not to be confused with the Picture Puffins of today) were conceived and launched in World War II, and the editor, Noel Carrington, commissioned experts in such subjects as *Trees in Britain*, *The Story of Furniture* and *About a Motor-Car* to write simply and directly about them. But read the opening of *Printing*:

> This book is produced by 'Letterpress' printing in five colours. There are many other processes of printing, and we are going to tell you, and show you by drawings, something about them.
> But first we must get back to the beginning, for we cannot understand or do anything well without knowing in the first place the ideas of the people who have done the best work in the past.

Today neither of those two paragraphs would be considered necessary; the reader can go straight to the nub of the matter with the next sentence that makes you start thinking about the subject itself:

> Before printing was thought of, the only way to make a book was to write it all out by hand.

The earlier opening now sounds both off-putting and condescending. The response from any thoughtful reader would surely be, 'If you're not going to tell me about printing, why do

you think I have taken the trouble to start reading your book?'
Compare the robust opening of a book about conservation
written by three members of the *Blue Peter* team, obviously
experienced in communicating with their audience:

> Humans have been living on this planet for two million
> years, but it is only in the last couple of hundred that we
> really have made a mess of it. Before it is too late, people
> have to change their ways.

There is a world of difference between the 'we' of the first book
and the 'we' of the second.

There have been changes, too, in the second half of the
twentieth century in the speed with which knowledge accumu-
lates and, most markedly, in the way it is transmitted and
stored. You have only to watch preschool children using
computers to realise this. Whatever your specialist knowledge
of a subject, you must keep up to date with, or have access to,
the most recent research, and you must be aware of the
methods by which the subject is being taught.[2] As with fiction,
it may appear that the short text for the youngest children is
easy to write, but you really have to know an awful lot about a
subject before you can reduce it to a series of accurate simple
statements, and put them in an order that allows the reader to
understand how they are connected.

It really is not so important how you acquired your knowledge – whether you have an academic doctorate, have spent
years observing the habits of a now endangered species, or have
always practised a particular and rare skill – the vital talent is
to know your subject so well that you are quite certain which
aspects of it need to be understood first by the beginner. A
logical shape to the material is as desirable as the shape of the
story for a picture book or novel.

A book that illustrates all the features of a good information
book for children is *The Way Things Work* by David Macaulay,
with Neil Ardley. David Macaulay is both writer and illustrator;
Neil Ardley, according to the acknowledgements, 'provided all
the technical text and shared his vast knowledge of the subject

---

[2]A helpful study of how children learn from books is Margaret Meek's *Information
and Book Learning*

with tremendous patience and enthusiasm'. The book's blurb suggests it is suitable 'for all ages'; reviewers put its age level as 'eleven up'. It is large in format, having the appearance almost of an encyclopaedia, but it is also very inviting, the mass of material in its 384 pages carefully organised in four sections, each divided into self-contained double-spreads dealing with one topic and illustrated with such verve that you feel its creators couldn't bear to waste a centimetre of space. The text begins:

> To any machine, work is a matter of principle, because every-thing a machine does is in accordance with a set of principles or scientific laws. To see the way a machine works, you can take the covers off and look inside. But to understand what goes on, you need to get to know the principles that govern its actions.
>
> The machines in this and the following parts of *The Way Things Work* are therefore grouped by their principles rather than by their uses.

There's no 'we are going to tell you'; it is assumed the reader is seriously interested, and the writer is equally serious in getting straight on with the job of making clear the rules by which he is working. But in case any reader should be worried that the work involved may be too difficult, romping across the bottom of the page comes an endearing mammoth, drawn in light-hearted style, to whom the reader has already been introduced by a mock title-page in eighteenth-century fashion reading:

> ... from my own sketchbook a highly personal account of several INVESTIGATIONS into the principles & workings of various *MECHANICAL MACHINES* brought to light during the CAPTURE, DOMESTICATION & subsequent EMPLOYMENT OF THE GREAT WOOLLY MAMMOTH being wholly free from the confusion of COMMON SENSE ...

Each of the principles is prefaced by a story of the mammoth, observed by the chronicler in a ridiculous situation which illus-trates the principle. So the mammoth throughout acts not only as an inducement to go on reading (he is a very likeable char-acter), but as reassurance to the reader who is more familiar with story lines than scientific explanations. Cunningly drawn into the book, this reader may suddenly find the working of a nuclear reactor clearly comprehensible.

The logic by which the writers' immense subject has been divided into four parts – the mechanics of movement, harnessing the elements, working with waves, and electricity and automation – also helps to make the material less daunting, and the connections that bring together wheelbarrow and bottle opener, tap and combine harvester, keep the reader constantly surprised and entertained.

What distinguishes this book (which took three years in the making) is the *idea* behind it, the humour with which it has been drawn and written, the thought that has gone into its organisation, and, above all, the enjoyment both writers seem to have in telling you how things work. It is this irresistible enthusiasm that publishers look for in writers of this kind of book. Here the writing of the technical text is plain and direct; specialist words are used, but the meaning is clear from the diagrammatic illustrations which fill at least half of every page. Printing, for instance, is described thus:

> The printing press, as its name implies, prints by pressing paper against an inked plate. Large printing presses are rotary machines in which the printing plate is fitted around a cylinder.

The mammoth stories, by contrast, are told in a consciously literary and humorous style:

On the conveying of messages
While on a mammoth watch in the mountainous southern area, I was asked for some advice in the matter of communication between remote villages. It appeared that the age-old system of conveying messages – which relied on catapulting couriers from one place to another – was critically threatened by a shortage of both volunteers and also paper. After inspecting the catapults and calculating certain distances and elevations, I devised a completely new system. Instead of relying on dwindling manpower, I suggested that the messages could be carried through the air in the form of stones ...

The technical aspects of the system worked perfectly. However, I had completely overlooked the villagers' atrocious spelling. So frequent were unintentional insults that all forms of communication eventually ceased.

And there the other voice takes over, to explain how modern telecommunications work.

61

If you want to write non-fiction, look first at the books already on the library shelves, then submit your ideas to a publisher with a sample of your style. Don't develop your ideas too far before you have found an interested publisher. The publisher should be more familiar with market needs than you are and, if impressed by your style, will probably want to work with you from scratch on the development of any possible book.

Poetry

In the last decade the publishing of poetry for children, in the form of single-poet collections or anthologies, has flourished and when the selectors for the 1991 Signal Poetry Award[3] met to make their final choice they had already considered over 130 books published during that year. The prize went to Anne Harvey for her anthology *Shades of Green*, and the judges commended it as a model for would-be anthologists.

So if you are compiling an anthology, have a look at Anne Harvey's book – and remember that she started collecting poems while at school and began making hand-written anthologies at the age of twelve. You can check what themes have already been covered by consulting the library of Young Book Trust at Book House, 45 East Hill, London SW18 2QZ. There you will find a copy of every children's book published during the preceding two years, and the cumulative list of titles and subjects is held on a database. (The book themselves, after two years, are transferred to the Renier Collection at the Bethnal Green Museum of Childhood.) You can also consult the Poetry Library at the South Bank Centre, Royal Festival Hall, London SE1 8XX, which houses the Signal Poetry Collection and runs an information service.

When you are collecting poems, it is important always to go back to their first appearance in print if you wish to use any in your anthology. If the poem is still in copyright – that is, if the poet is still alive, or if his death, or the poem's posthumous publication, occurred less than seventy years ago – permission will be required for the inclusion of the poem, an acknowledgement printed, and a fee paid.

[3]An annual award of £100

Until 1 January 1996, copyright subsisted for only fifty years from the end of the year of the author's death, but on that date legislation was passed to bring British practice into line with that of other members of the European Union. This legislation was not applied retrospectively, but the work of authors who died between 1926 and 1945 came back into 'revived copyright'. Permission to grant the use of such work lies not with the original publisher but with the current copyright holder, usually – but not always – the author's Estate.

Your publisher may look after the permissions application for you or you may have to do it yourself. Whichever way this is done, it is wise to enclose a photocopy of the material with your request to use it, so you can be sure the words are reproduced exactly as the poet intended.

Publishers are always interested in the voices of new poets, but many people still seem to believe that four-lined, rhymed verses about Jack Frost are all that children can appreciate. This is far from true, as any good teacher will tell you, and it is worth looking at some recent publications to see what is being written for children by poets like Ted Hughes, Mike Harding (winner of the 1996 Signal Award) or James Berry.

It is also worth remembering that Anne Harvey received her first commission as a result of writing to the publisher of a book she admired, *A Puffin Quartet of Poets*, and suggesting a follow-up. *Poets in Hand, A Puffin Quintet of Poets*, was published in 1985, twenty-seven years after the anthology that inspired it. If you have an idea for a book of poetry, try it on a publisher whose list features similar books that you have enjoyed.

6. Taboos

Most of us no longer feel so sure that we know what frightens children as that remarkable woman, Mrs Trimmer, who took a firm stand against fairy tales in the early nineteenth century. But the adults who provide children with books today (whether writing, publishing or buying them) naturally take a very protective attitude towards their readers. Even if we are uncertain whether books have any lasting effect on the reader or not, no one wants to take any risks where children are involved, and both writers and publishers are probably over-sensitive about this. Mrs Trimmer, in her magazine *The Guardian of Education*, suggested that fairy tales 'usually make deep impressions, and injure the tender minds of children, by exciting unreasonable and groundless fears.' And one of her correspondents felt that 'Cinderella' should be kept from little children because it painted 'some of the worst passions that can enter the human breast, and of which little children should, if possible, be totally ignorant; such as envy, jealousy, a dislike to mothers-in-law and half-sisters.' Today we have much more practical concerns. We are worried that what children find in stories may place them literally in physical danger.

Safety

It is sad to think that no one now could take the risk of publishing a story like Edward Ardizzone's *Lucy Brown and Mr Grimes*, written in 1937 and reissued (with some tactful changes to the text) for the artist's seventieth birthday in 1970. Lucy, an orphan, meets an old man in the park, becomes his friend, and finally is invited to stay with him always. Today it is doubtful a child would be allowed to go to a park alone. Stories now include implicit messages of not speaking to

64

strangers, of being careful about going near stray dogs, of never accepting lifts home, of keeping always within safe distance of friends or parents. Must strangers always be shown as suspect?

The difficulty for writers is that so many of the best plots are about running away, going off on your own, showing initiative, in other words doing all those things that coincide with flying the nest, letting go of the adult reins – all of which, in the contemporary scene of rising crime figures and social deprivation, may lead to danger. If this is the kind of story you are writing, my advice would be to keep faith with its original impetus, making it credible (because otherwise it won't be read anyway), knowing how your characters would speak and behave, but to look at all those superficial details that might suggest to a child a course of action whose results could be unexpected and fatal. I am thinking of easy access to the medicine bottle ('Dad's room was in a mess and he'd spilt a bottle of aspirin all over the floor'); fireworks in pockets; playing on building sites ('we'd found a secret place ...'); farming tractors on slopes.

Language

Yet language remains the cause of the greatest trouble. Children's publishers are as opposed as anyone to censorship, but they have to be very wary of language and subject matter that could be thought objectionable by the adults who stand between writer and reader. Writers should be, and are, free to write anything that is neither libellous nor obscene, but with the writer of children's books the publisher has a responsibility to point out anything that may cause the intervening adult to see that the book never reaches the eyes of children.

Most often it is language that makes parents complain. This is odd, for at a time when the book is not much valued as a possession, you would not expect such firm belief in the influence of the printed word. I don't know why, but there seems to be a deep-seated fear of some words. I have been shocked by the violent way adults react, as if the words themselves were evil – I think of a headmistress who told me quite seriously she had considered *burning* a book containing the notorious four-letter word that brought the publishers of the unexpurgated *Lady Chatterley's Lover* into the Old Bailey in 1960. At the same time, writers often react equally violently if asked by their publishers to change words for this reason. Children, they rightly claim, know these words already and how, in a moment of high drama, can you reproduce realistic dialogue without resorting to some form of swearing?

I think, as a writer, you have to be ready to discuss the problem with your editor if and when it arises. Your editor will certainly not just take a blue pencil to your wording. What you have to remember is that, if a parent does complain, it is neither the publisher nor the writer who is in the firing line, but the bookseller or the librarian who has the book on display.

Controversial subjects

Different decades produce different anxieties, different taboos. Today it is unthinkable that a children's book should arouse such controversy as Maurice Sendak's *Where the Wild Things Are* did in 1967. Published four years earlier in the USA, its notoriety ensured a public and very solemn debate on TV concerning the terrifying effect it would have on children's minds. Only when the children themselves got hold of it and laughed with delight at the Wild Things did the rumpus subside. But I suppose it is the thought of frightening children that most worries publishers, and the truth, we are told, is that no one can predict what will cause terror in the mind of one child but not in the next. The best advice for the writer comes from Sendak himself:

> Certainly we want to protect our children from new and painful experiences that are beyond their emotional comprehension and that intensify anxiety; and to a point we can prevent premature exposure to such experiences. That is obvious. But what is just as obvious – and what is too often overlooked – is the fact that from their earliest years children live on familiar terms with disrupting emotions, that fear and anxiety are an intrinsic part of their everyday lives, that they continually cope with frustrations as best they can. And it is through fantasy that children achieve catharsis. It is the best means they have for taming Wild Things.[1]

[1] Acceptance speech for the Caldecott Medal, 1964

Yet publishers today seem unwilling to admit that any subject is taboo in a children's book. Even World War II and the concentration camps have been treated in picture books, though both Art Spiegelman's *Maus: A Survivor's Tale* and Innocenti's *Rose Blanche* belong to that category of picture book which puts their readership among older children of twelve or so. By contrast, John Burningham's *Granpa* shows how even death can be introduced into a book for the very young. Never actually named in the text, Granpa's absence is only shown in the illustrations. Adult readers may weep at the sight of Granpa's empty chair on the penultimate page, but children apparently accept this philosophically.

Despite the empty chair, *Granpa* ends with a cheerful picture of the little girl who's been his companion in play pushing her doll's pram up the hill. And that, I think, is the answer to the question of happy endings. It has become almost a cliché that a story for children must end happily, but this is not always possible, or desirable. Everyone knows that some stories cannot end tidily: something has changed, people have changed, nothing can be quite as it was at the beginning. But with a children's book it is important that any underlying fears or mystery be resolved, so that the story finishes on a note of hope – however much has been left for the children to imagine about what happened next.

7. Attitudes and Assumptions

The children's book divisions of publishing houses tend to be staffed mainly by women. A knowledgeable reviewer of children's books, Margaret Meek, once suggested that they are characterised by a real care for what children read. 'One of the unacknowledged facts of women's success in writing, publishing and promoting books for the young,' she wrote, 'is the genuinely co-operative concern they have shown for this age group, despite the more obviously competitive ethos of their paymasters.'[1] While women are in the majority, the men who have entered this field of publishing are equally committed. The late Sebastian Walker set up his own publishing house devoted solely to children's books. By paying children's writers on the same scale as their adult counterparts, and by offering them the same standard of promotion and marketing as applied to adult books, he raised the profile of children's writers in the 1980s beyond anything they had known before. In the academic world it is, for the most part, men who have in the last decade established children's literature as an acceptable branch of learning and research. The two annual lectures on this subject are endowed in memory of Patrick Hardy, editor and publisher, and H.J.B. Woodfield, the founder of *The Junior Bookshelf*, one of the first critical review magazines started in 1936.[2]

Concern about what children read extends beyond the subject-matter of their books to the way writers use language. At first, children read words for their literal meaning, which is why editors put such emphasis on the choice of words (not to restrict vocabulary, but to ensure its accurate use), the consistency of punctuation (again, to facilitate understanding), and

[1] *The Signal Selection of Children's Books 1988*
[2] Details from Young Book Trust

grammatical rules that help avoid any ambiguity in meaning. Quickly children learn that words can be used ironically, in their opposite sense. What can only be learned by experience is the understanding of how some words and phrases represent attitudes and assumptions by the writer that an adult recognises and interprets accordingly.

The power of words

Words are powerful, as an advertisement used by the NSPCC acknowledges:

> If a child has been physically abused you can see the bruises. But verbal abuse can be just as damaging. You don't see the scars, but they are there and some of them never heal ... When you discipline your child, it's important to criticise her action rather than criticising her as a person. In other words, saying 'That was a horrible thing to do', instead of 'What a horrible girl you are' ...

Verbal abuse is easy to spot; what I would call verbal 'putting down' is insidious, often unintended, often taking the form of simply ignoring certain people or aspects of society. The reverse is also characteristic of writing for children: each writer will have moral beliefs that are promoted, consciously or unconsciously, in the development of that writer's story. Peter Hollindale, a lecturer in English and Education, puts this more precisely than I can:

> ... writers for children (like writers for adults) cannot hide what their values are. Even if beliefs are passive and unexamined, and no part of any conscious proselytising, the texture of language and story will reveal them and communicate them ... It might seem that values whose presence can only be convincingly demonstrated by an adult with some training in critical skills are unlikely to carry much potency with children. More probably the reverse is true: the values at stake are usually those which are taken for granted by the writer, and reflect the writer's integration in a society which unthinkingly accepts them. In turn this means that children, unless they are helped to notice what is there, will take them for granted too.[3]

[3] *Ideology and the Children's Book*, 1988

Avoiding stereotypes

Sometimes an unthinking society needs a bit of a shake; in the 1970s children's book publishers had several. The first, ironically, came from the Women's Movement. In 1974 the McGraw-Hill Book Company in New York issued to its editors guidelines 'for equal treatment of the sexes' in all the company's non-fiction publications, suggesting that:

> Men and women should be treated primarily as people, and not primarily as members of opposite sexes. Their shared humanity and common attributes should be stressed – not their gender differences. Neither sex should be stereotyped or arbitrarily assigned to a leading or secondary role.

The guidelines were straightforward but created a furore that concentrated on some of the absurdities in Preferred Terminology. Although they had originated with a firm that specialised in teaching materials, they made children's publishers in London look even more carefully at books already under inspection in answer to a questionnaire circulated by the UK Children's Rights Workshop, which asked 'In how many books that you publish does a girl play a leading part?' Precious few, it had to be admitted; looking at children's picture books, the reader would find mothers at the sink or behind the buggy while the person at the wheel of the car was invariably father.

There was a lot of huffing and puffing, but the truth was that no one had noticed fiction falling behind in its reflection of life as many children knew it. Between 1971 and 1976 the number of children with working mothers (that is, working outside the home) increased by one third.[4]

Guidelines should never be regarded as rules, but they can be helpful as a reminder not to take things for granted, not to perpetuate clichés in thinking and writing. The McGraw-Hill list of substitutes for *Man*-words may itself now have become a cliché, being taken for granted, but it would be unusual today to read 'Housewives are feeling the pinch of higher prices', the Preferred Terminology of 'Consumers (customers or shoppers) ...' having become the norm.

---

[4]This information comes from a children's book, *Growing up in the 1970s* by Nance Lui Fyson, 1986

Much more serious than their treatment of women, children's publishers' perceived élitism and their blinkered view of society were criticised by many in the 1960s and 70s. It was claimed that editors all belonged to the same stratum of society, being white, middle-class, from homes where books and reading were taken for granted. Writers, it was claimed, belonged to a similar, exclusive, inward-looking group of people, who wrote either in a literary tradition familiar to the few, or in what they patronisingly considered the language of the playground. Both publishers and writers were jolted out of their complacency and made to look at the children who were entering the classroom. It was immediately obvious that certain children – notably those who were neither white nor whole in body or mind – were hardly even mentioned in books. One publisher, visiting a children's hospital in Australia and admiring the library, was reproached by a child in a wheelchair who said she'd never seen a picture of anyone like her in a book. Another child, also in a wheelchair, rushed off to fetch a book of symbols, and there was the sign used on public buildings to indicate access to wheelchairs. The publisher returned to London determined to put this right – and did.

The rush to redress the balance resulted in books *about* black and disadvantaged children, books *for* them, and a search for writers among ethnic and other minority groups that could leaven the mix of children's reading material. Some books were successful, others less so, perhaps because they had been created for a purpose rather than from imaginative impulse. Illustrators were taken to task for merely adding a 'token' black face to their drawings. That criticism was probably justified; more hurtful was the judgement that white writers should not portray black characters. Ezra Jack Keats, an American artist, whose picture book *The Snowy Day* caused black children in the United Kingdom to hug themselves in joy at identifying with the figures in the illustrations, was the subject of critical attack in New York.

The situation today is better, I hope. Undoubtedly writers of books for children remain predominantly white but now are as likely to come from a non-bookish background as not, and they will have grown up in a multicultural society that they take for granted. I was told by editors that, although the mix of characters is now more likely to reflect society as it is, adults are still reluctant to accept the description of a child who is black or disabled in any situation that could be construed as negative. In other words, a writer starting on a story of two children, one the hero the other the anti-hero, must think carefully when giving the child characters physical features. Before you protest about this, just think about the frustration of being in a helpless situation for any length of time. If you have experience of being disabled, even temporarily, you will know how frustration builds up over the simplest activities, like pushing open the door of a shop. Time, surely, will change this, but for the moment we are still not treating *all* children primarily as people (to refer back to McGraw-Hill's timely guidelines), and fiction has to take account of this.

The concept of 'politically correct' (PC) language also orginated in the USA in the late 1980s with those who believed certain phrases could reinforce various forms of prejudice. The phrases were all related to different 'isms' – ableism (a dismissive attitude towards the disabled), ageism (disdain for the very young or the very old), Eurocentrism (bias in favour of Western values), classism (prejudice of one social class towards another), lookism (bias in favour of one standard of beauty, usually Western), weightism (bias against fat people). It is easy to make fun of the extremes to which such guidelines can lead ('I went to a special school; for people with teaching difficulties'), but to call their use censorship is only to fuel the resentment that has motivated their creators. The disabled have enough to put up with; if they, or their carers, wish to be identified in a certain way, writers and publishers should take notice.

You, as a writer, cannot keep your values hidden. As Peter Hollindale said, they will be revealed in everything you write. When you are starting on a book for children, it is worth spending time examining your values, knowing that these are what you are passing on to another generation whose circumstances may be very different from yours. If you have no doubts, then press ahead, concentrating on the words that will most exactly reproduce the scene and the characters that are in your mind. It is then up to your editor to make the first response, to say what impression has been transmitted to the *reader*'s mind. Where the two don't match – that is where the editorial work begins, and at the same time it is the editor's responsibility to point out words that may be misunderstood, that are discriminatory or may cause offence, just as it is the editor's job to look out for any words that could be thought libellous and therefore the subject of legal action. (This is very unlikely to occur in a book for children, but your contract should include a clause which allows your publisher to carry insurance against any legal proceedings resulting from libellous statements.)

From what publishers and writers have told me, I know they believe that one of the things literature does – and should do – is to give readers confidence in their own individuality. Anything that undermines this confidence, by suggesting a child of certain race or gender, or with some physical or mental abnormality, is of lesser worth, should be avoided. This does not mean censoring words or scenes that show such a child being *treated* in such a way by people who know no better; it does mean looking carefully at the context in which words like 'sambo' are used, and thinking about how they will be understood by a child reading them in print for the first time.

8. Contracts, Writers' Organisations and Literary Agents

Even authors of long experience say that parting with your finished manuscript, putting it in the post to your chosen publisher or agent, is like sending your child off alone into the wide world at the start of the first school term. You have indeed parted with something of yourself, and now what you have written is to be shared with a reader whose job is to look at it critically, considering it not just on its literary merit but with an eye to its selling potential in the marketplace. No wonder you feel apprehensive. Before sending off your manuscript, do remember to make a copy for yourself. If you use a word processor, of course, you will have the text on disk, but if you work on an old-fashioned typewriter then you will need to make a photocopy. Whichever the case, the text should be typed with double spacing, every page numbered (this is important) but preferably not stapled to its neighbours. If you want to include something that is irreplaceable (a sample of artwork, for instance), don't entrust this to the post but make a photocopy. Publishers cannot assume responsibility for loss of unsolicited manuscripts. Remember also to send stamps for the manuscript's return, should it be rejected. Your accompanying letter need not be lengthy; it should explain why you have chosen to send your work to this publisher or agent (showing that you have some knowledge of the publisher's list or the agent's other clients) and perhaps mention the readers whom you think it may interest. The *Writers' and Artists' Yearbook* suggests sending a preliminary letter of enquiry; I would recommend doing this only if you want to propose a book of non-fiction.

Do not be worried or surprised if you hear nothing (apart from an acknowledgement) for several weeks. I know the horror stories that are told of lost manuscripts, of publishers taking months to make up their minds, but I do believe these are the exceptions to the usual procedure. Each manuscript is considered with the same care, but priority has to be given to work on books that have already been accepted for publication, so the reading of unsolicited material often lags behind, especially at holiday times of the year when departments may be short-staffed. Most children's publishers receive about fifty manuscripts every week and the arrival of each is recorded meticulously, together with its fate. (I remember few tears in my office, but my secretary was once heartbroken when she thought a manuscript really had disappeared. It turned up safely, having been transferred as more suitable for the adult department. That division goes on causing problems.)

If your manuscript comes back to you, it will probably be accompanied by a courteous but bland letter, saying that your work is 'not suitable for our list'. This may be irritating, but unfortunately publishers cannot afford the time to explain in detail what they found unsatisfactory when your manuscript is only one of the thousands they see every year. Try a second publisher, and a third; remember Richard Adams, whose *Watership Down* was rejected by several major publishers before becoming a bestseller in the 1970s. Remember Kenneth Grahame, an established writer, whose *Wind in the Willows* was turned down by his regular publisher, and received luke-warm reviews before it began to sell, never stopping since.

The recession of the 1990s has been bad for everyone, especially for booksellers and their customers like librarians and teachers who rely on public money, and for publishers. This means that it is even more difficult for publishers to accept work from unpublished authors, because they have no proven track record of sales. As Judith Elliott, children's book publisher at Orion, said when she started this comparatively new list in 1992:

> The economic climate means we can give them [new writers] less grace, less time to get established. The pressure is on to succeed straight away. The whole idea of serving an apprenticeship in print has gone. The second and third books from a new writer are crucial: you just can't wait for the 'breakthrough' title that's going to do it.[1]

[1]'Filling a niche – or getting stuck in the ghetto?' by Mary Hoffman, *The Bookseller*, 4 September 1992

Although, four years later, Judith admits that selling books is no easier, she still has faith that, for a new writer of fiction with real talent, the future is promising. The marketing of a book, however, has become vitally important.

At the same time, publishing depends on new talent and has always done so. If you receive a letter of even minimal encouragement, take heart, and accept every bit of advice you are offered. Perhaps you will be asked to put aside the manuscript you have submitted and to try something else. Do this; it's hard to give up something you have laboured over, but I am sure that every published author has, somewhere, a manuscript that has been hidden away on a publisher's suggestion, a manuscript that may sometime become a book but that for the moment should not see the light of day.

The contract

If, instead of your self-addressed package, you receive a letter with an offer to publish your work, then in today's hard times you have done well. The offer will consist of an advance, a sum against which the royalties on sales of the book will be set, and a royalty, that is, a percentage of the book's price. Since the price will be lower than that of an adult book (see p. 5), though the royalty percentage may be the same, the actual amount will be less, and the advance on a children's book accordingly lower – in the region of £500 to £2,000. This advance may be payable half on signature of the contract and half on publication (probably nine to twelve months later).

Adult books can command much higher advances than children's books partly because their sales pattern is different – an adult book of universal interest may be linked to some notable event or anniversary that ensures large sales on publication. But remember that the enormous advances you read about in the press are for the very few – and may be boosted by the amount a newspaper will pay for the right to serialise, for example, the memoirs of someone in the public eye.

Both advance and royalty may be lower on a first book than a publisher would offer to an established author, for these amounts will be based on the publisher's prediction (guesswork) of how many copies will be sold within a certain period.

The advance may also take into account the likelihood of the publisher selling other rights in the material. For example, if the publisher has a paperback imprint then the editor concerned will also have considered your manuscript and the advance will reflect the predicted sales of a paperback edition; however, the advance may then be paid in thirds: on signature of the contract, on hardback and on paperback publication.

You may think a publisher's contract looks too complicated for you to understand, but your editor should be willing to go through it clause by clause with you, explaining the significance of each. The *Writers' and Artists' Yearbook* offers advice on the clauses that are essential in any publishing contract and the particular points that should be examined carefully – for instance, when will your book be published? Can the publisher sell the rights in the book to someone else without consulting you? When will you receive royalty statements? It is worth looking at the section entitled 'Publishing Agreements' before the contract is signed.

Writers' organisations

You may still feel uneasy about such a daunting document. If you have received a firm offer in writing for your manuscript, then you can become an associate member of the Society of Authors (84 Drayton Gardens, London SW10 9SB), who will advise you. Associate members pay the same subscription (£70 for the first year, £65 thereafter; this may be reduced for authors under thirty-five) and are entitled to the same benefits as full members. Founded over a hundred years ago, the Society has about 6,000 members and its Children's Writers and Illustrators Group (membership normally confined to those with two published books) has been active in raising the status of children's writers. As an associate member, you can get a specialist opinion on your first contract. This can be invaluable, since the contract may set precedents for those that follow, and you will be better off than consulting, say, your usual legal adviser who may be unfamiliar with the intricacies of the publishing business.

The Writers' Guild of Great Britain (430 Edgware Road, London W2 1EH) offers a similar service on similar terms, but in addition to the annual subscription full members pay a supplementary subscription based on their earnings.

If you feel that you would rather not spend money on professional advice about your contract, I should not be too worried about trusting your publisher. If the advance is less than it might have been, this means at worst you have to wait longer for the income from sales to arrive. Of course, as an ex-publisher, I must be biased, but it is only common sense for a publisher to make a reasonable offer for a first book. If the book is a success, there will be plenty of other publishers interested in the second and it will soon be obvious whether the contract for the first was fair. Ah, you will say, but there was an option clause ensuring that the second book should be offered to the same publisher. Look carefully to see whether the option clause specifies 'on the same terms' and, if it does, suggest amicably to your publisher that this phrase be deleted, since neither of you can know whether the first book will be a commercial success and whether the second book will be as good.

Literary agents

Not all the literary agents in London deal with children's writers, but some are specialists in the field. You can find them in the *Writers' and Artists' Yearbook*, where they state very precisely the commission they charge (on average 10%) and the kind of material they can consider. For instance, Caroline Sheldon (who, like some other agents, has been a publisher of children's books) gives her requirements as:

> Full-length MSS (manuscripts). General fiction, women's fiction, and children's books (home 10%, overseas 20%). No reading fee. Synopsis and first three chapters with large sae in case of return required initially.

If you submit your work to an agent and it is accepted, then the agent will probably know exactly which publisher is most likely to take it on and may be able to get you a better deal than you could on your own. One agent I consulted said she would be more interested in someone who wanted to make a career of writing than the author of a single text.

On the other hand, if you have thought carefully about the publisher's list on which you would most like to appear, you may save time by going to that publisher direct.

I know it is sometimes said that, in the adult field, publishers pay more attention to manuscripts submitted via an agent, but in my experience this does not apply to manuscripts written for children.

Public Lending Right

As soon as your book is published and copies are available for loan in the public libraries, you will become eligible for payment on library loans – provided you are resident in the United Kingdom or Germany. If any other name, say that of the illustrator, appears with yours on the title page, then you will both have to agree on how the payment is divided. To register for PLR, write for the necessary forms to Bayheath House, Prince Regent Street, Stockton-on-Tees TS18 1DF.

9. Being Published: Editors and Others

'No project is undertaken with greater hope and a deeper sense of insecurity,' said an author, 'than the writing of a book.' But now your work is finished, your hope is fulfilled, the contract is signed and you can feel secure in the knowledge that the manuscript has started on its way to becoming a printed book. Several people will be involved in its gestation during the usual period of nine months or so. The first person you meet, whether in person or on paper, will be your editor, whose official title may be 'Acquiring Editor', 'Sponsoring Editor', even 'Editorial Director' or 'Publishing Director'. She – I am using the feminine pronoun because the majority of children's book editors are women – will have chosen to publish your manuscript because she believes in it, and she will already have presented her case for it to an Editorial Committee, probably with estimated calculations of its production cost, an opinion of its likely readers, and a forecast of its potential sales. You can be sure that from the start she wants to make everyone concerned with designing, producing, promoting and marketing the book as enthusiastic about it as she is, and to give it every possible chance of reaching its readers.

Your editor

The editor has dual loyalties and responsibilities: to you, the author, to make certain your text is as true a representation of your talents as it can be, and to the people who have the job of getting your book into the hands of its appropriate readers. The marketing people who are going to take your book into shops, supermarkets, schools, libraries, or wherever, need all the help the editor can give them in identifying those unique qualities that distinguish it from all the other books on offer. Publishing is a business, and in a free market where everyone, including teachers,[1] has the right to choose what books they buy with their limited funds, competition is fierce.

Working practice varies from firm to firm, but normally your editor will be eager to meet you as soon as possible and to discuss the manuscript in detail with you. I know there is a common belief that editors love to rewrite, but I have rarely met one who did. What your editor is passionately interested to discover is whether the responses she has made to your story are what you expected (or hoped for), whether the effects you worked so hard to make have succeeded as you intended, whether your feeling for the characters has been transmitted through your words to her as you wanted. In discussing the manuscript like this, you and she will recognise any weaknesses at once, and ways of strengthening the structure will occur to you without agonising over what 'revising the manuscript' might mean. Often it is a matter of cutting rather than expanding, of substituting words rather than providing long explanations. I have sometimes worried myself into the ground over telling an author about a scene which didn't seem to me to work, only to watch that author smile and say, 'Do you know, I wasn't quite sure about that myself. Now, what shall I do about it?'

The working relationship that develops between writer and editor is very important, but it depends on the writer having absolute trust in the editor, whose roles encompass those of midwife, guardian, adviser, supporter, and (it is hoped) friend. Some publishers' contracts include a clause stipulating that no changes be made to the text without the author's approval, but this should be unnecessary if you trust your editor and should be regarded merely as a precaution against a change of editor if the publishing firm is sold into new hands.

Before your manuscript is passed to the designer, it will be copy-edited. Some firms have copy-editors on the staff, others use freelances, and their job is to standardise spelling, check

---

[1] 'Teachers in the UK have the freedom, subject to budgetary limitations, to select and order any books they wish to use in their classrooms and libraries. This freedom is valued by all concerned with education.' *The Supply of Books to Schools and Colleges*, Report of the David Committee, 1981

punctuation, look for any inconsistencies in the continuity of the story. Any major problem (you may, in a fast-moving story, have inadvertently occupied your characters for eight days in one week) will be referred to you for settlement. Spelling is a question of house style: in this book, for instance, 'ise' endings are used in preference to 'ize' because this follows the house style of A & C Black. Ask your editor for a copy of the house rules, and if you don't like them, say so. A useful guide is the standard book on the subject, *Copy-editing* by Judith Butcher. The book makes it very clear that the author's wishes are paramount, but the copy-editor's responsibility is 'to remove any obstacles between the reader and what the author wants to convey, and also to save time and money by finding and solving any problems before the book is typeset, so that production can go ahead without interruption.'

Announcing publication

The first announcement of your book's publication will be made about six months ahead in your publisher's catalogue (generally produced in spring and autumn of each year). This catalogue, of course, will be read by the adult buyers of children's books, most of whom are faced with a deluge of similar catalogues and know only too well the clichés of blurb-writing. 'Vibrant' pictures, 'enchanting and original' stories, 'gentle' humour – the bookseller has heard it all before. *How, how* is your editor to put across in 150 words or less the essential quality of your work, pinpointing its age-group, persuading the buyer of its difference from the rest? Not easy – which is why you will have received a questionnaire asking for a brief biographical sketch, information about aspects of your book that might interest the media, your opinion of its main selling features. Anything you can tell your editor about the inspiration for the book, its connection with a local landmark, its autobiographical detail, will be helpful – so don't regard the questionnaire as an intrusion of privacy, or a chore to fill in, and do follow the instruction about supplying a photograph of yourself, preferably an unposed shot showing you looking happy. Old and young readers all want to know what the writer looks like.

Several thousand copies of the catalogue will be despatched to all those people who might place orders for your book ahead of its publication: retailers, chains of bookstores, wholesalers, book clubs, educational and library suppliers, libraries themselves, and so on. The catalogue will be followed by a smaller circulation of the jacket (or cover), and an even more exclusive distribution of paper-bound proof copies of the text. (These are expensive, but there are among the sellers of books dedicated bibliophiles who will read and assess everything they can. However, this takes time. How many books can you absorb in a week?)

Meanwhile, your editor will have been allocated perhaps half an hour to address the sales force at its biennial conference. In that time she will have to fire every representative there with enthusiasm for your book and all the others (maybe fifty in all) to be published in that season. The room will be filled with people from the UK, from other parts of the English-speaking world such as Australia, New Zealand and South Africa, and from places like Holland and Sweden where books in English are read, and they will be listening for two days on end to editors describing their hopes for the next Booker prize, the latest sex-and-shopping blockbuster, or handbooks for weight-lifting as well as weight-losing. It's like running a four-minute mile with only one chance to succeed. Sales Directors sometimes set an exercise for this trial of oratory. Reduce to one sentence the nature of the book, your reason for publishing it, the inducement for a bookseller to stock it!

The jacket

So you will understand that, next to the catalogue announcement, the jacket, which each sales representative will carry on that one selling expedition for each season, is the vital sales aid. The picture and the blurb on the jacket or cover of your book have to achieve two things: persuade the adults to buy it and entice the children to read it. The blurb is perhaps the easier to get right: just a hint of the story line to arouse curiosity (never give the whole story away), a broad indication to the adult of the age-group, and a 'puff' to show the publisher's pride in the book (and to give a bit of help to the lazy reviewer). It is prudent to avoid using words like 'here', which suggest the publisher has arrogantly forgotten some readers may live on the other side of the world, or 'this year', which make the publisher look foolish if the first impression of the book stays in print for more than one year.

The illustration of the jacket may be more difficult. If you have written a text for a picture book, then you will already have been introduced to the illustrator and the book will be developing as a collaborative effort involving artist, writer, editor, art editor and designer. The subject for the cover will evolve naturally from the artist's ideas for the inside of the book, and you will have begun to experience what everyone describes as the unique pleasure of seeing the interpretation an artist brings to your words.

If you have written a novel then obviously you will know it so well you will have a picture in your mind of what should go on the cover. This may not coincide with what the artist finds in the story, and neither may match what is considered a 'selling' jacket. Your editor will of course consult you, probably sending you several 'roughs' of the artist's proposals. Many contracts now include, as a matter of course, a clause giving the author right of approval of the jacket, but in my experience, with a first book, it is wise to take your editor's advice on the views of the Sales Department. If a book doesn't clear this first hurdle of getting the sales representatives' backing, it may have few chances of reaching the children who should be its readers.

The designer's work on the jacket is just as important as that of the artist and the blurb-writer. Most books stand on shelves with only their spines showing: title and author's name must be clearly visible, and it is no use hoping black lettering will show up on, say, a brown tree trunk, no matter how integral the latter is to a Rackham-esque picture that runs across the spine.

Choosing the typeface

Legibility is vital in all parts of a children's book. This was the firm belief of one of the great typographic designers, John Ryder, who wrote:

A page in a book must not look like a collection of letters. At least it should look like a collection of words, at best a collection of phrases. To achieve this, not only must the right letter-design for the language and text and format be chosen, but it must also be used in a way that allows the easy flow, and therefore recognition, of phrases.[2]

In picture books and books for the beginning reader this 'flow of phrases' is especially significant, and the designer will try to arrange the text so that breaks in the sense come at the end of lines, where, if you were reading aloud, you might pause for effect or to take breath. This sometimes takes much ingenuity, and if you are asked, at proof stage, to consider a change to the text so that it can be read more easily, or so that a lone word at the top of a page (known to the printer as a 'widow') can be avoided, be prepared to discuss this. Both editor and designer have one end in view: to make your text as clear to read and to understand as possible.

If you look at the type on this page you will see that the space between the words varies from line to line, because each line runs to the same width. Occasionally this will mean that the words almost run together. For the reader who is just starting, the words will be more legible if the space between them is uniform. The designer can specify this, but each line becomes slightly different in width and the right-hand margin will be uneven. This is 'unjustified' setting and you can see it on the page reproduced overleaf from Robin Kingsland's book *Free With Every Pack*.

Similarly, the spacing between the lines (the 'leading') is important for legibility and can often compensate for the small size of type. Clearly, if you make the type very large, you run the risk of having to break words at the end of lines, which looks ugly as well as causing confusion in the reader's mind. An editor will try very hard to avoid word-breaks between pages (particularly on a turn-over) and may ask you to consider changing a word for this reason.

The editor may also request a special typeface in a book for younger children. The 'a' and 'g' in this book are not the forms used by children learning to write. Some teachers think it is

[2]*The Case for Legibility*, Bodley Head, 1979

When he was five, Oswald had begged his parents for a pet. They said that they would get him something quiet, that was cheap to feed, and didn't need much exercise.

It took Oswald ten years to realise that he had been given a pet carpet.

It was on the day that Oswald's father had the carpet put down that Oswald started being *really* mean.

21

confusing for beginning readers to learn two versions of these letters, and you will find many texts printed in a typeface which has a script 'ɑ' and 'ɡ' as on the facing page.

Some publishers prefer to use double quotation marks in younger books to avoid confusion with the apostrophe, moving to single quotes as the reader grows older. American publishers use double quotes for all books. If you have an opinion on this, talk about it with your editor.

Pricing the book

When the text of your book has been set, the proofs corrected and the jacket finalised, the crucial decision must be made about the number of copies to be printed. It is this figure that brings the publisher success or disaster, for the print quantity dictates the unit cost, on which the published price will be calculated, and this in turn directly influences the number of copies that will be bought. Print too many, to keep the price down, and you may end up with the cost of keeping the books in the warehouse overtaking any margin of profit. Print too few, and the higher price may result in the books staying in the warehouse just the same.

With an established author there are track records of previous books' sales to give some guidance. With a new author the publisher, or editor, is working in the dark – although marketing colleagues may have taken soundings from booksellers and others and will be able to advise. But it is usually a matter of the editor, who has faith in the book and the writer's talent, backing her own judgement with a confidence that she must pass on to everyone in the long chain between creator and reader.

Whatever the quantity, certain fixed costs have to be paid, and perhaps the clearest way of showing how a book is priced is by analysing its cost in terms of percentages:

1 Booksellers' discount   **42%**
This is an average: discount varies from 35% upwards given to most UK booksellers (the carriage is paid by the publisher) to 50% and over on overseas sales, on which the publisher does not have to pay the freight for books supplied.

2 Costs of production   15%
Printing, paper and binding, together with some fixed
charges – the cost of separating the artwork for a
picture book or a jacket into colour printing plates, or
the cost of setting up the text of a novel – which can be
spread over the total print quantity.

3 Author's royalty   10%
To help keep the price low, in order to establish a children's book that may go on selling for many years, the
author may be asked to accept a smaller starting royalty
(for example, 7½% rising to 10% after the sale of a
certain number of copies). Since the discounts given to
booksellers began to increase, the royalty is now often
paid on the money received by the publisher, with the
percentage proportionally increased.

In the case of a children's picture book this royalty
may be shared between author and illustrator (whether
artist or photographer).

In addition, the author will of course receive royalties from the sale of other rights in the book.

4 Publisher's editorial, design and promotion costs   8%
Rent, rates, heating and lighting of office premises;
salaries and pensions; telephone, fax, postage costs;
catalogues, advertising, posters and leaflets; exhibiting
at Frankfurt and Bologna Book Fairs. Unlike adult
books, each of which may have money allocated to its
promotion, children's books are usually promoted
jointly – by means of catalogues, posters, book fairs,
etc.

5 Selling, distribution and warehousing costs   15%
Maintenance of sales force travelling round UK to visit
bookshops, and their counterparts working in the
overseas markets of Australia, Canada, Europe, New
Zealand, and South Africa; administration of sales,
computer, invoicing and accounts departments
(including royalties); maintenance of warehouse to
store books before they are sold; carriage on books
sold in UK.

6 Margin of profit   10%
This must cover payment of interest on borrowed
money, tax, and investment in future publishing

projects. It may be eroded if not all the copies printed
are sold, or if more copies than expected are sold at
high discounts.

Total 100%

Some of these items have to be paid for in advance of antici-
pated sales, and others are costs that will be incurred whether
or not that anticipation is correct.

Costs of production
Printers allow their customers a certain amount of credit, but to
stay in business they must expect their invoices to be paid
within 60 or 90 days. Since publishers need to have books in
their warehouses at least 40 days before they can publish and
make their first sales (so as to give time for the pre-publication
orders to be sent out to booksellers), they usually have to pay
for production before cash begins to flow back from the booksellers. The booksellers in their turn expect a minimum of 30
days' credit (in the case of overseas booksellers, because of the
distances involved, this may extend to 180 days).

Author's royalty
The author's advance against royalties will probably be paid
half on signature of the contract for the book and half on publication.

Publisher's costs (editorial, distribution, etc.)
These basic costs have to be paid regardless of the number of
copies sold. Predicting turnover is guesswork: if turnover (that
is, revenue from sales) falls below the level predicted, then the
percentage covering selling and warehousing goes up.

Profit margin for investment
No publisher can survive by standing still. Money is always
needed for exploring and investing in new projects which may
not become books for years to come.

As you can see, it may be some time before the publisher
recoups the production costs and begins to make a profit, so the
publisher will be as anxious as you are to find out what are the
chances of selling the rights in your book to an American or
foreign-language publisher. This job is the responsibility of the

Rights Manager – again, very often a woman – who will already have taken part in discussions about your book and will be planning possible strategy.

Selling rights

Sending out reading copies of a book (which often are not returned) can be costly, so much preliminary work is done at the two annual international book fairs. The Bologna fair, usually around Easter, is for children's books only; the fair in Frankfurt, about October, covers books of all kinds. Publishers from all over the world display their new publications and at half-hourly appointments from dawn to dusk talk non-stop about the new authors, the new ideas, the new writing they have to offer. Your Rights Manager, selling your book to new audiences, will be using all her expertise, her knowledge of overseas markets, and her understanding of the foreign publishers whose tastes and enthusiasms in books will be familiar to her.

Depending on the length of book and its nature, you may not hear immediately whether any foreign rights have been sold, but within a few months there may be good news. If an American publisher buys the right to publish in New York, then you may be asked to consider changes to the text for the American market. Spelling has to be adjusted: 'maneuver' (US) for 'manoeuvre', 'practice' (verb) for 'practise', 'practise' (noun) for 'practice'. American punctuation has different rules: the closing quotation mark is always placed *after* commas and full stops, whereas British practice puts it before.

Other changes will always be referred to you for approval and your editor will be on hand to help if you do not feel happy with what is proposed. When I made a retelling of some of Aesop's fables the American publisher sent a list of suggested changes. Of course 'skirting board' must become 'baseboard'; yes, some rephrasing was a distinct improvement. But should 'ass' be changed to 'donkey' because, in North America, 'ass' is a taboo word for 'arse'? After thinking about it, I told my editor in London that, though I didn't want to cause embarrassment to any adult using the book in a classroom, perhaps American children should know that there was an animal distinct from the donkey and this was what appeared in the first written records of the fables. The message was passed on; the American publisher courteously agreed to my original wording and, so far as I know, there has been no trouble. When this same book was translated into German, I had a very apologetic telephone call from my editor. In the introduction I had explained, perhaps a bit too flippantly, that nothing would have induced me to read Aesop as a child because the children's classics of my childhood looked so dauntingly 'worthy'. The German publisher, whose list I knew and much admired, said this simply would not do. Out of respect for that publisher's judgement I agreed to the substitution of a more scholarly preface explaining the nature of the fable. (I still feel this was maybe unfair to my young German readers.)

When you do not know the language into which your book is being translated you really have to take the translator's intentions on trust. You can be sure that if there has been any problem in the past your editor is likely to know about it and will want to ensure it doesn't happen again. American publishers usually visit London on their way to Bologna or Frankfurt and like to meet the British authors whose books are on their lists. Take every opportunity you can of talking to your editors from other countries; it is always useful to know about the response of readers in far-off places.

Marketing and publicity

Last of all, but certainly not in importance, come the marketing and publicity staff who will be making certain that everyone of significance in the children's book world has heard about your book or received a review copy. Again, the distribution of review copies is expensive and there is no guarantee, at least in the national newspapers, that there will be space for even a one-line mention of the book. Review space for the most part goes to adult books, unless there is some sensational story attached to a children's book – generally about the author – that will secure public interest. At the Christmas season there will normally be a round-up of children's books suitable as presents, and occasionally an author of a children's book (usually dead) will be the subject of a feature article, but mostly the regular reviewing of children's books is done in the specialist journals. So don't expect reviews on publication day; they *will* come, but months afterwards, from journals like *The School Librarian* in the UK or *The Horn Book Magazine* in the USA.

Children's books rarely make news, but your publisher will (with your approval) have been in touch with the local newspaper and local radio and TV stations. What journalists always want is a story, a peg on which to hang the news of your book's appearance. Any snippet of gossip about the local origins of your book will be pounced on. Of course the press are irritating: far too interested when you don't want your privacy invaded, completely dismissive often when your publisher is trying to create interest in what you do want to tell. If, after everyone's efforts, nothing happens on publication day – don't despair! Your turn will come. Put all your energy into the *next* book, which by now should be well on its way.

10. And Now?

Publishers have only very imprecise information about the readers of the children's books they publish. Even the bestseller lists reveal only which titles are bought in largest quantities, not who is buying, certainly not who is reading them. The sales figures that appear on the publisher's computer screen or the author's royalty statement show how many copies (usually in hundreds, sometimes in thousands, hardly ever in millions, unlike TV viewing figures) have been sold to retail and whole-sale 'outlets' but what happens to the books after that can only be guessed. If a particular agency or wholesaler is dealing with one section of the market, say schools, then that figure may be more informative, but on the whole publishers have to rely on anecdotal evidence from teachers, librarians and parents about the children reading their books.

The author, on the other hand, often has the great satisfaction of hearing from the actual consumer, the young reader who writes a letter. Though some schools in the UK copy the American habit of making 'Writing to an author' the project of the week, most letters seem to be written on personal impulse, with only minimal help from an adult. Children usually address their letters care of the publisher, who forwards them, for no publisher would ever divulge an author's address (although this may sometimes be found in a reference book). You can learn a lot from children's letters: they are usually direct, honest, and they deserve a reply. A brief acknowledgement is probably all that can be managed or is even needed, but it will be much appreciated.

Probably what *you* want most is to see your book on show in the local bookshop and with any luck you will. If it isn't there, don't panic; ask for it and see what the bookseller says. There was a copy in stock but it's been sold (good); no sales representative from the publisher has been seen lately (bad); it can be ordered (good); it's out of print (oh, no). If the answer is unsatisfactory, talk to your editor. There may be a straight-forward explanation. Small booksellers cannot keep every new book in stock, nor would publishers want this if the bookseller does not foresee any demand. It is a waste of time and money if books sit on the bookseller's shelves unsold and then are returned to the publisher's warehouse for credit (the publisher can't send them back to the printer).

Booksellers' information usually comes from Whitaker's list-ings on microfiche or CD-ROM (see p. 5) but Whitaker rely on publishers for keeping that information up to date and occas-ionally there are mistakes. If a bookseller tells you your book is out of print, write to your publisher immediately. The inform-ation may be incorrect, through no fault of the bookseller.

Royalties

Your guide to your book's sales is your royalty statement, which should come to you twice a year, on dates specified in your contract. It is worth studying this carefully and asking your editor to go through it with you if you cannot follow it. You will not receive any money with the statement until the advance has been earned, and the figures will show how quickly that sum is being reduced. If, after two years or so, you notice that the sales are very low, or even down to nil, ask your editor whether a reprint is planned. In hard times the decision to reprint has to be taken with some care, for increased costs of production may mean a higher published price. If your publisher decides not to reprint, and there is no other edition still in print, then ask for the rights in the book to revert to you. It may be a few years before anyone shows interest in reviving the book again, but if you have retrieved the rights you will be in a better position to negotiate a new edition.

Now that you are, as your editor will hope, writing a second book you will discover that your work is expanding to take in other aspects of being a writer. First, you will have to keep an eye on the business side of things, as I have just mentioned. This is when you may find membership of a writers' organisation useful (see p. 77), or you may consider asking an agent to represent you. In either case, your editor's advice will be helpful. Second, your publisher will ask if you would be willing to speak to children in a school or library, or to talk to a group of interested adults. If you are accustomed to public speaking, you will need no advice about this, but if the prospect worries you, take heart. Publishers are often asked to do this kind of thing and I was always nervous before the event, but I found some rules given to me by a parson almost foolproof. Never write out exactly what you are going to say, he told me; that way you will lose all spontaneity and never lift your eyes from your script. Think it all out in your head; write down only the bare plan, under headings, of one word if possible. If you have, say, divided your talk into six topics, write your six headings in large capitals on a sheet of paper (or six small cards, if you prefer) so that you have to glance down only now and then to remind yourself of what comes next. Look at the back row of your audience; if they start scowling, stop and ask if they can hear. It's like holding one end of a skipping rope which is slack to begin with – then, suddenly, there is a pull at the other end and you realise the audience is responding. You're away!

The difficulty about being an author is that the one thing most children want to know is how you do it, and whereas an artist can draw endlessly with lots to show for it, writing can't be demonstrated in the same way. So think up all the anecdotes you can: where your ideas come from, how you found a publisher, how long it took to write your book. Take along proofs on which you can show what has been corrected and why. Children love to spot mistakes; a first proof of a jacket on which the colour was faulty, a sample of your handwritten work with words crossed out, this kind of material will enliven your talk. Visits to children can be rewarding both in ideas for new books and in making new readers, for recommendations from friends are the best advertisement for a new writer. So spare as much time as you can for supporting children's book events. Your publisher will look after the arrangements and see that your name is added to the directory of writers and illustrators held by Young Book Trust.

And now – you are embarked on your writing career and I wish you all the luck in the world. Without writers for children today, there will be no readers tomorrow.

Postscript

In the four years since I wrote this book the book trade has been going through a rough time. The recession in consumer spending that began in the early 1990s affected bookshops as dramatically as other high-street stores, but for a while it seemed that children's book sales were still buoyant. This led to an increase in output, and inevitably the market, saturated with books, became almost stagnant. In publishers' offices staff were made redundant, and publication plans cut back. Looking for a way to stimulate sales, the publishers abandoned the Net Book Agreement – by which they had set the price at which their books were sold. Booksellers believed the price-cutting this allowed would put small, independent booksellers out of business but most of the price-cutting was confined to supermarkets and one chain of bookshops, suggesting that whatever makes people buy books it is not primarily their price.

It had been predicted, however, that the price of books would go up (to allow for the higher discount required by the booksellers) and this did happen with adult books. Significantly, the change in the price of children's books has been minimal. What *has* changed on the children's book scene is the number of books that have flooded the market. When checking the statistics on page 5, I was shocked to discover that in June 1996 there were over 54,000 children's books in print compared with 30,000 in June 1992. What this means for publishers is that – with far less public money around for libraries and schools to spend on children's books – the emphasis is on finding new buyers and readers, new outlets beyond the traditional bookshop, rather than looking for new writers.

In this book you will have noticed that most of the advice I offer is based on the assumption that the editor has the authority and the time for giving lots of attention to discovering and nurturing the new writer. Sadly, in these more difficult times, you may not find this is so, and it will be a matter of luck whether, at your first attempt, you meet a publisher or agent who can afford to spend time working closely with you on a first story or novel, never mind devoting a year (as the editor did in the example I quoted on p. 28) to coaxing a beginning author's talent into flower.

All this made me think hard about the situation of the unpublished writer. What I have learned from established authors is that the greatest need, when you are starting off, is for someone on whom you can try out your work. Most people don't want to show their first efforts to families or friends, knowing that the closer the relationship the more reluctant will the reader be to say anything that sounds like criticism. Sometimes even successful writers are quite hurt that their own children won't read their books – but surely this is understandable. No one wants to face the possibility that something created by someone dear to you is not absolutely perfect.

One answer is to join a creative writing group. You may find a local group that meets informally to read, listen and discuss. Or there are professionally run courses, some residential, which will cost you money and time, but which may give you that extra start or the confidence to go on working at your manuscript until it proves publishable.

There are, of course, any number of organisations that offer writing courses, but only a few provide specialist workshops in writing for children. Among the latter, the following have been recommended to me:

The Arvon Foundation runs residential courses, lasting four or five days, at three centres. Details from the Arvon Foundation at Lumb Bank, Hebden Bridge, West Yorkshire HX7 6DF; at Totleigh Barton, Sheepwash, Beaworthy, Devon EX21 5NS; and at Moniack Mhor, Teavarran, Kiltarlity, Beauly, Inverness-shire IV4 7HT.

The City Literary Institute runs courses in London that follow the academic terms with weekly sessions. Details from 16 Stukeley Street, London WC2B 5LJ.

The Taliesin Trust runs residential courses in Wales on similar lines to the Arvon courses. Details from Tŷ Newydd, Llanystumdwy, Criccieth, Gwynedd LL52 OLW.

I asked two established authors whether they thought such courses could be useful and they both spoke warmly of their experiences. Rose Impey, now the author of many best-selling books, joined an Arvon course at Hebden Bridge in 1984 and says that making the decision to go gave her the psychological lift of suddenly feeling a writing career might really be within her grasp. Later that year her first work was accepted and she's never looked back since.

> I think in the early days I was like many aspiring writers and pretended to look down on creative writing courses, but even at the time I knew that was as much out of fear as arrogance. When I finally pushed through that fear and attended an Arvon course I realised immediately how much I could learn not only from the tutors but from the other students. But even more important was that the courses played a vital part in my taking myself seriously as a writer.
>
> I still attend courses from time to time. I always find them stimulating and use them nowadays to widen my writing by choosing poetry, a new medium to me, or drama.

Malorie Blackman, who had her first book published in 1990 and went on to win the W.H. Smith Mind Boggling Books Award[1] in 1994 with *Hacker*, agrees.

> When I first decided that I wanted to write for children I had no idea how to go about it, no idea where to start. This is when a good course is so invaluable. I started a 'Writing for Children' course at the City Lit in Holborn. The tutor – a published author herself – spent the first term discussing picture books, the second early readers and in the final term we covered novels for 8 plus.
>
> The next year I did the follow-on – a 'Writing for Children' workshop. Now we brought in our work to be read and criticised by others in the group. It wasn't just the feedback we received that made it so worthwhile, it was the fact that

[1]Sadly now discontinued, this was an annual award of £5,000 for the best paperback novel for children aged between nine and twelve, the winner being chosen from a shortlist of reviews written by children of the same age-group

every publishing success or failure could be shared with others in the same boat, others who could empathise and advise. The group was too large for everyone's work to be read every week, but I found I learned just as much from listening to other people's stories as I did from presenting my own work. One particular clever thing our tutor did was to insist that someone else read your story for you. She said, quite rightly, that you learned more from listening to your story than by reading it aloud yourself. It was instructive to learn which bits were read effortlessly, which were struggled over, which stood out and which were just unnecessary verbiage.

My definition of a good course is one run by someone with practical experience in writing – either as a published author or as a children's book editor. And a good course is one where the group is supportive yet not afraid to express their views. I always tried to make sure that I'd say what I liked about a story before I said what I disliked! I can honestly say that the 'Writing for Children' workshops set me on the right road.

So, despite all the problems facing publishers and booksellers as the millennium approaches, the beginning writer need not feel despair. Hard times may mean fewer publishers producing fewer books, but for the writer with a distinctive voice, a good story to tell, and the determination to go on revising and polishing until the manuscript is as good as it can be, the future is bright.

Books Mentioned in the Text

Books for children

Alice's Adventures in Wonderland, Lewis Carroll, Macmillan, 1865

Bella's Dragon, Chris Powling, Blackie, 1988

The Blooding, Nadia Wheatley, Viking Penguin, 1987

The Blue Peter Green Book, Lewis Bronze, Nick Heathcote & Peter Brown, BBC Books/Sainsburys, 1990

The Borrowers, Mary Norton, Dent, 1952

Bows Against the Barons, Geoffrey Trease, Lawrence, 1934

Can't You Sleep, Little Bear?, Martin Waddell & Barbara Firth, Walker Books, 1988

Charlie and the Chocolate Factory, Roald Dahl, Allen & Unwin, 1967

Cloudy, Deborah King, Hutchinson, 1989

The Dead Letter Box, Jan Mark, Hamish Hamilton, 1982

Dear Nobody, Berlie Doherty, Hamish Hamilton, 1991

Dogger, Shirley Hughes, Bodley Head, 1977

Dog's Journey, Gene Kemp, Collins Children's Books, 1996

The Donkey's Crusade, Jean Morris, Bodley Head, 1983

The Eighteenth Emergency, Betsy Byars, Bodley Head, 1974

Each Peach Pear Plum, Janet & Allan Ahlberg, Viking Kestrel, 1975

The Famous Five: Five have a mystery to solve, Enid Blyton, Hodder & Stoughton, 1962

Father Christmas, Raymond Briggs, Hamish Hamilton, 1973

Free With Every Pack, Robin Kingsland, A & C Black, 1988

Fungus the Bogeyman, Raymond Briggs, Hamish Hamilton, 1977

Gentleman Jim, Raymond Briggs, Hamish Hamilton, 1980

Granpa, John Burningham, Cape, 1984

Hacker, Malorie Blackman, Doubleday, 1992

The Hobbit, J.R.R. Tolkien, Allen & Unwin, 1937
The Iron Man, Ted Hughes, Faber, 1968
Just So Stories for Little Children, Rudyard Kipling, Macmillan, 1902
Krindlekrax, Philip Ridley, Cape, 1991
Let's Go Home, Little Bear, Martin Waddell & Barbara Firth, Walker Books, 1991
The Little Pink Pig, Pat Hutchins, Julia MacRae Books, 1994
Lucy Brown and Mr Grimes, Edward Ardizzone, OUP, 1937, revised ed. Bodley Head, 1970
Maus: A Survivor's Tale, Art Spiegelman, Penguin, 1987
Midnight Blue, Pauline Fisk, Lion, 1990
Nothing to be Afraid Of, Jan Mark, Kestrel, 1980
Oi! Get Off Our Train, John Burningham, Cape, 1989
The Owl Service, Alan Garner, Collins, 1967
A Parcel of Patterns, Jill Paton Walsh, Kestrel, 1983
The Pigman, Paul Zindel, Bodley Head, 1969
Poets in Hand: A Puffin Quintet, ed. Anne Harvey, Penguin, 1985
Printing, Harold Curwen, Penguin, 1948
A Puffin Quartet of Poets, ed. Eleanor Graham, Penguin, 1958
Rose Blanche, Roberto Innocenti & Ian MacEwan, Cape, 1985
Rosie's Walk, Pat Hutchins, Bodley Head, 1968
Shades of Green, ed. Anne Harvey, Julia MacRae Books, 1991
A Stranger at Green Knowe, L.M. Boston, Faber, 1961
Sunshine, Jan Ormerod, Viking Kestrel, 1981
Swallows and Amazons, Arthur Ransome, Cape, 1930
The Tale of Peter Rabbit, Beatrix Potter, Warne, 1902
Thunder and Lightnings, Jan Mark, Kestrel, 1976
Watership Down, Richard Adams, Rex Collings, 1972
The Way Things Work, David Macaulay with Neil Ardley, Dorling Kindersley, 1988
The Way to Sattin Shore, Philippa Pearce, Kestrel, 1983
When the Wind Blows, Raymond Briggs, Hamish Hamilton, 1982
Where the Wild Things Are, Maurice Sendak, Bodley Head, 1967
The Wind in the Willows, Kenneth Grahame, Methuen, 1908
Winnie-the-Pooh, A.A. Milne, Methuen, 1926
The Witches, Roald Dahl, Cape, 1983

You and Me, Little Bear, Martin Waddell & Barbara Firth, Walker Books, 1996

Books for adults

Babies Need Books, Dorothy Butler, Bodley Head, 1980, revised ed. Penguin, 1995

Copy-editing, Judith Butcher, CUP, 1975, third revised ed., 1992

The House in Paris, Elizabeth Bowen, Cape, 1935

How Texts Teach What Readers Learn, Margaret Meek, Thimble Press, 1985, revised ed. 1988

Ideology and the Children's Book, Peter Hollindale, Thimble Press, 1988

I'm the King of the Castle, Susan Hill, Hamish Hamilton, 1970

Information & Book Learning, Margaret Meek, Thimble Press, 1996

Read with Me, Liz Waterland, Thimble Press, 1985

The Reluctant Reader, Aidan Chambers, Pergamon, 1969

Twentieth-Century Children's Writers, ed. Tracy Chevalier, St James' Press, 1978, third ed. 1989

Writers' and Artists' Yearbook, A & C Black, annual publication

Index

paperback
  editions 7–9
  rights 77
picture books 16–25
poetry 62–3
protecting children 64–5
Public Lending Right 4, 79
public speaking 95
publicity 91–2

quotation marks 87

racism 71–2
reading schemes 25
review journals 12
rights, selling 89–91
royalties 5, 8, 9, 76, 88, 89, 94

sales conference 83
satire 44–5
school book fairs 9
schools, books in 9, 10, 55
series publishing
  for beginner readers 25–6, 28–30
  of non-fiction 57
  for teenagers 49

sexism 70
Signal Poetry Award 62, 63
Smarties Prize 21, 43
W.H. Smith Mind Boggling Books Award 98
Society of Authors 77
spelling, American 90
stories
  for beginner readers 25–7
  for independent readers 28–9, 30–4
  for picture books 17–20
style 15–16, 68–9

taboos 64–7
teenage novels 45–54
translations 54

vocabulary 24, 27, 32

Whitbread Award 45
Writers' Guild of Great Britain 77
writing, children's 30

Young Book Trust 62, 95